Thanksgiving

The Pilgrims' First Year in America

Glenn Alan Cheney

Glenn Cheney

New London Librarium

974.482
Cheney

Published in 2007 by
New London Librarium
P.O. Bx 284
18 Parkwood Rd.
Hanover, Conn. 06350
www.NLLibrarium.com

First Edition

Printed in the United States of America

Cheney, Glenn Alan
Thanksgiving: The Pilgrims' First Year in America

Includes bibliographic references

1. Pilgrims (Plymouth Plantation) 2. Indians of North America—First contact with Europeans

ISBN:
978-0-9798039-1-8 [paperback]
978-0-9798039-0-1 [hardcover]

Other Books by Glenn Alan Cheney

Journey on the Estrada Real

Journey to Chernobyl

Frankenstein on the Cusp of Something

Passion in an Improper Place

They Never Knew: The Victims of Atomic Testing

Acts of Ineffable Love: Stories by Glenn Cheney

This book is dedicated to

every immigrant

who has come to America,

and to every American

who has welcomed them

with grace and assistance.

Contents

Foreword

This book is nonfiction. We like to think of it as "a true story." We have stuck to the facts as best we have discerned them, and we have tried to reflect the truth. Truth, however, is an elusive, if not impossible, ideal. The truth isn't so much in the objective data as in the human experience. To say that the *Mayflower* crossed the Atlantic in sixty-six days and that people got seasick would be a lie of omission, a belittling of an experience beyond the imagination of modern people. The two writers who related the crossing were guilty of that same omission, but their spare descriptions hardly mean the passengers experienced the trip as no more traumatic than an extended church service.

In our attempt to reflect the truth of the Pilgrim experience in that first year in America, we had to walk a fine line between fact and imagination. The facts alone would deny the bigger truth, but imagination necessarily explores the unknown and inevitably stumbles into places that just don't exist. In general, therefore, we stuck with the facts and left imagination to the reader. Now and then, however, we apply a little conjecture, suggesting a scene within the scope of probability. These passages are either tagged with a qualifier, such as "probably" or "may have" or "no doubt," or are obviously imaginary descriptions of what we can be pretty sure happened. The occasional quotations from the Geneva Bible, appearing here in italics, were not uttered at the moments being described in this narrative. Rather, they are inserted as illustrations of the kinds of religious thoughts and prayers that typically filled the minds of these devout people.

The matter of truth also comes up against the question of "whose truth" and "how much truth." Historians often disagree in their interpretation of facts. We could argue forever, for example, on the question of whether the technology of the Indians was inferior to that of the Europeans or was simply appropriate to their environment and social structure. We could argue over whether Indian medicines — the inner bark of the dogwood for colds, skunk oil for the purging of the bowels — were any more effective than

Europeans cures.

On other issues, exhaustive inclusion of details could bore or confuse the reader, hiding the forest in the trees. Generalizations simultaneously deny and simplify the truth while bringing it within reach and grasp. It is hard, for example, to explain the complexities and variations in English churches. It's hard to say something general about several Indian tribes as they existed over the course of centuries. Generalization always lies, but how else can we step beyond specifics and into interpretation?

We hope our simplifications, generalizations, qualifications and conjectures bring the reader closer to rather than farther from the truth. We have tried to tell a true story, a story of human experience. We hope the story tempts the reader's imagination and that the reader succumbs to it.

We put a lot of thought into how we should refer to the people who lived in New England when the Pilgrims arrived. Some descendents of these people take offense at the term "Indian" while others accept it as the term that has, over the years, simply become the word that is most widely used and is used without intent to offend. We also found many native Americans offended at the exclusionary term Native American.

In our attempt to come as close as possible to the Pilgrim and Indian experience, we decided to begin the story using the term that the Pilgrims used: savage. Neither the Pilgrims nor the author of this book have used the term in its modern sense, the one associated with savagery. Rather, it meant, to them, people who lived in the wilderness. That's how they saw the people they couldn't see, the ones they heard in the forest, people who shot arrows from behind trees, made smoke in the distance, and walked their dog on the beach. We use that term in this book until the Europeans actually meet the Americans. Thereafter, we identify these people either as Indians or, more commonly, by the name of their tribe — the Pokanoket, the Massachusetts, the Nauset, etc. Here and there we do refer to the "Wampanoag," a term that came about later in history, to refer to several allied tribes in the Cape Cod area.

Those are the terms of this book. We hope the overall effect is one of deep respect for the Europeans who came to America and for the Americans who welcomed them. Both groups acted with courage, wisdom, and understanding. They recognized that cooperation, generosity, and trust would serve them better than suspicion, prejudice, and conflict. The relationship was one of life's infinite varieties of friendship, and it worked well. It was a good start toward a country that would have a lot to learn.

Prologue

It's hard to track back through the events of history to figure out why, in 1620, 102 people packed themselves into
a ship and sailed off to live on a distant continent. How far
back should we go? At the very least we should step back
a century and some to 1488, and we should go to Spain.
King Ferdinand of Aragon and Queen Isabella of Castile y
Leon had political reason to betroth their daughter Catalina
to Prince Arthur, the eldest son of King Henry VII. Allied
with England, Spain would be better able to attack France.
King Henry, a Tudor, liked the idea of someone attacking
France, but he also liked the dowry that would come with
a princess. He also liked the idea of marrying royalty. As
the first Tudor to rule England, he needed the recognition
of a foreign monarchy to shore up his shaky claim to the

throne.

The young couple weren't quite ready for marriage — he was two, she three — so it wasn't until 1501 that a fleet of Spanish ships delivered the sixteen-year-old Princesa Catalina and half her dowry to Plymouth, England. She and Arthur married in November. A few months later, they both took ill with infection. Arthur died. She didn't. The widow Catalina claimed that the marriage had never been consummated. The pope believed her. By special dispensation, he allowed her to betroth Arthur's little brother, Henry. Little Henry was twelve.

Despite the nod from God, young Henry protested, quite likely on the advice of his father, who was looking for some other way to keep the half of the dowry he'd already received. His son's marriageability might be more profitably applied elsewhere in the political squirmings of sixteenth century Europe. Things changed significantly when Isabella died. A complex balance of power shifted, and Ferdinand no longer needed to marry his daughter into English royalty. He was content to keep the half of the dowry they hadn't yet lost. Henry VII still hoped for the other half, so he held on to the girl until something could be worked out.

Before Catalina could return to Spain, the situation squirmed again. Big Henry died, and little Henry, the eighth, rose to the throne. Two months later, in 1509, with the blessing of the pope, he married Catalina. The people of England called her Catherine. The marriage worked for a while. Henry went off to war on the mainland, leaving his Catherine as Regent of England. While he tried to make France English, she tried to beat some sense into Scotland. Their shared interest in hegemony and war, however, wasn't enough to sustain their marriage. Catherine was bearing children at a reasonable pace, but they were dying at almost the same rate. Only one survived. To the dread of Britain, it wasn't a boy. It was a girl, and her mother gave her the most Catholic name she could think of — Mary. But Henry didn't need a Catholic daughter. He needed an English son lest the kingdom one day fall into the hands of a woman.

What he needed was a better wife. Divorce wasn't so easy in those days of devout Catholicism. One solution, he thought, might be to have the pope reconsider whether his marriage to his brother's widow had really been valid in the first place. If it wasn't, then perhaps a divorce or annulment could be granted. The pope didn't like the idea, perhaps because Catherine's nephew Carlos, the last so-called emperor of the Unholy Hardly-Roman Nonempire, had just sacked Rome and was closing in on the Vatican.

Meanwhile, in Germany, a young man named Martin Luther was asking the pope similarly difficult questions. It wasn't about divorce. He was a monk. Marriage wasn't his problem. His problem was the relationships between man, church, and God. As he saw it, a lot of religious responsibility ought to be shifted from popes and priests to individuals. Individuals, he said, should be responsible for their own repentance, their own actions and beliefs, their own souls, and their own relationships with God. In other words, they had to do a lot of thinking and praying for themselves, at least to the extent that God allowed. Repentance had to come from their hearts, not their wallets. This revolution in religious thought began when he nailed to a church door in Wittenberg his list of ninety-five "theses," or statements he wished to defend. That was in 1517. Luther's questions loosened a thread in the tightly woven tapestry of Catholicism. As it began to unravel, the pope's patent on religion in Europe began to break up.

As for the Henry's divorce issue, the pope could not bring himself to papally annul what had been papally approved, especially with Carlos's army at the Vatican gate. Henry's next best idea, then, was simply to start a new church that could recognize certain necessities. In 1534, with Henry's encouragement, Parliament created the Church of England (two centuries later known as the Anglican Church) with Henry himself as its Supreme Head. As such, he could, and did, grant himself a divorce. He dispatched his ex-wife/ex-queen to a suburb and within a fortnight married Anne

Bolyn, leaving the people of England whispering about the nature of good and evil, right and wrong, marriage and divorce, and who truly had the right to impose God's will on Man. Some said the pope. Some said the king.

And some said neither.

Henry's subsequent execution of two wives, his devotion to war, his mistresses, divorces, drunkenness, and obesity did little to persuade the English that a king at the head of a church was any more moral than a pope in that position. Henry did manage to provide the Y-chromosome to a child, a sickly boy named Edward. When Henry died in 1547, he left England in the hands of a nine-year-old, the last of the legitimate Tudor males. Five years later, before really taking power, the boy died of tuberculosis and the measles.

By written will, Edward left his throne to a cousin, Lady Jane Grey, but she had little claim to the Tudor line. The real choice was between Catherine's Catholic daughter, Mary Tudor, and Anne Bolyn's daughter, Elizabeth, who was raised under the Church of England. Or, as those of the Catholic persuasion saw it, England could be led by Mary, daughter of the king's only legitimate marriage, or Elizabeth, illegitimate daughter of the king's paramour.

Technical legitimacy won out over the politics of religion. With more popular support than Queen Jane, Mary had the queen beheaded after just nine days on the throne. Mary then reigned for five years, from 1553 to 1558. During that brief period, she tried to return Catholicism to its former power and glory. All she succeeded in doing, however, was bankrupting the nation, losing its last territory on the mainland, and raising tensions between the Catholics and Protestants of England. Having three hundred Protestants burned at the stake for heresy did nothing to smooth relationships. All it did was earn her a memorable nickname: Bloody Mary.

Bloody died in 1558. By default, her half-sister, Elizabeth, rose to power. Elizabeth reigned for forty-five years, just long enough to clean up the political and economic mess that her vain and reckless father had left behind. She tried to quell the hatred between Catholics and the worshippers of the Church of England, but her defense of Protestantism elsewhere in Europe made it clear which faith she favored. She didn't do much to quell tensions among English Protestants, either. Worship outside the Church of England was prohibited but not prevented. Many ordained ministers trod a fine line between strict adherence to the Book of Common Prayer and sermons that suggested a different way of thinking.

Elizabeth never married. She lived until the end of 1602, when, for lack of successor, the reign of the Tudors came to an end. James Stuart, king of Scotland, succeeded her in 1603.

The early seventeenth century, then, found Catholics at odds with those of the Church of England, and those of the Church of England were at odds with Protestant dissenters, among them the Puritans and the Separatists. (Typical of religions everywhere, the definitions of these groups were by no means consistent, tending to vary from group to group, especially among dissenting groups who were striving to establish distinct beliefs.) The Puritans accepted the principle of the Church of England but wanted to purify it of its showy ceremonies, clerical vestments, and other remnants of papism. They sought these changes from within the established church.

The Separatists, a tiny group of loosely affiliated churches which never really identified themselves as "Separatist," were essentially Puritans who saw less hope of reforming the Church of England. Separatists weren't so sure that the Catholic church and Church of England weren't following parallel paths to the same fires of Hell. Whether they followed king or pope, their souls, they feared, would be doomed. They didn't want a Church *of* England any more than they wanted a Church *of* Rome. The very name implied that the church was *subservient to* or *belonging to* England. For them, 2 Corinthians was pretty clear about what they had to do: *Come out from among them and be ye separate, saith the Lord.*

What the Lord said, Separatists did, so they separated, devising their own church, a church where "church" meant neither an institution nor a building but a gathering of worshippers. They didn't *meet in* a church. They *were* a church. In their church, the clergy wore simple clothes and devoted more energy to sermons, less to ritual. Their church didn't have priests but a pastor. There was a difference. For one thing, the Bible said nothing about priests. For another, priests were appointed from outside the church. Then they came in and took over all interpretation of scripture, all communication with God. Separatist pastors, on the other hand, were more like shepherds, merely guiding their flocks in their interpretation and prayer. The pastors were ordained and thus might know a little more than their congregations, but they were as fallible as any other human.

Separatists didn't worship saints or celebrate saints' days. They didn't sing prescribed hymns, recite creeds, or chant prefabricated prayers. They didn't kneel to pray unless they felt like it. They thought it repugnant for a groom to give a bride a ring. They considered the celebration of Christmas and Easter idolatrous. Their holy days were the Sabbath, the Day of Humiliation and Fasting, and the Day of Thanksgiving and Praise. The Sabbath, Sunday, was, of course, a weekly day of rest and worship. The other two *ad hoc* holy days were declared as necessary. They declared a Day of Humiliation and Fasting when a downturn in circumstances indicated God's displeasure with unrepented sin — sin they were stuck with due to Man's inborn moral imperfection. When things went suspiciously well, they declared a Day of Thanksgiving to thank God for overlooking the inevitable sins of an undeserving people.

The Separatists believed that they could worship in a home as well as in a cathedral. The flexibility of worship space fit well with the threat of fines, arrest, torture, and death by hanging. With no identifiable church buildings, no central organization, no structured hierarchy, no sign out front, and no supreme leader besides God, they were hard to identify, hard to catch in the act, hard to eliminate as a threat to the Church of England. Each congregation took care of itself and reported to no higher authority. These isolated organizations worked well. Their cellular structure would eventually evolve into that of the Congregational Church in America, where each church is independent and the minister of a given church has risen as high as he can go. Hierarchically speaking, a Congregational pastor was, and still is, on a par with a pope.

But you wouldn't want to call a Separatist pastor a pope. The Separatists saw the Church of England's rejection of an omnipotent pope as a big step toward Heaven on Earth, but the appointment of a king to serve in the place of a pope just stepped back toward authoritarianism and its inevitable companion, corruption. The Separatists could not accept any authority standing between them and God. They didn't let a professional do their praying. They read the Geneva Bible and other books and applied their knowledge to religious decisions. They didn't think they were thinking for themselves. That would be impossible in a universe controlled by God. But they made every effort to figure out what God wanted them to think.

The Geneva Bible was known as such because it had been translated and published in that city. The Geneva Bible's primary translators were English Protestants who had fled their country under Mary's bloody reign. Their translation of the New Testament came out during Queen Mary's time. The Old Testament translation came out a few years later, during Elizabeth's reign. The margin notes of these editions made it clear that the satanic beast that was to emerge from the pit of Hell, the beast foreseen in Revelations, would be the pope himself. The pope had a rack for people who thought like that. Other side notes suggested the fallibility of kings. King James didn't like that part, and he had a gallows for people who did. He disparaged the Geneva Bible and ordered a new translation, a beautifully poetic version that came to bear his name.

The Separatists believed the Geneva Bible and accepted its notes. They recognized the possibly of error in translation, but generally they believed its every word, and if the word wasn't in the Geneva Bible, they didn't believe it. If their Bible didn't describe a ceremony, prescribe a prayer, mention a ministerial garment, or declare a holiday, they didn't accept it as part of their worship. The closest they came to recital of a prayer or the singing of a hymn was the recitation of a psalm, sometimes in melody, never in harmony, never with instrumental accompaniment. If they said the Lord's Prayer, they varied the words to fit the passion of the moment. They may have recited from Psalm 19: *The statutes of the Lord are right and rejoice the heart: the commandment of the Lord is pure, and giveth light unto the eyes.*

In the philosophy of John Calvin, the Separatists wanted to participate in the administration and theology of their church — an idea that ran contrary to papism, Roman or English. They wanted a voice in the election of their authorities— an idea that ran contrary to kings, queens, princes, dukes, marquis, barons, counts, viscounts, viceroys, earls, assorted lords, and landed gentry in general, not to mention priests, bishops, archbishops, sufragen bishops, archdeacons, rectors, vicars, and curates.

It would not be accurate to say that the Separatists wanted to choose their authorities. At most they might use their individual voices to try to express the natural hierarchy that God had intended. Together they might approximate God's will. This wasn't egalitarian democracy, but looking back, we might see the seed of it. These were the kind of people kings didn't like, the progenitors of people who didn't like kings. They accepted the role of king as absolute ruler, but only in the earthly realm. Matters of God, Heaven, and religion were of a kingdom beyond the king's.

The Church of England itself was not uniform in all parishes. In some villages, the congregations leaned a little toward Puritanism. In others, they stuck with the prescribed rules of worship found in the Book of Common Prayer. The Puritans, too, ranged from radical to conservative, and the Separatists, off on the fringe of the radical side, were still trying to figure out what God wanted them to do. Psalm 107 said, *Let them exalt him also in the congregation of the people, and praise him in the assembly of the elders.* God was clear on that. But did he prefer a certain posture for prayer? Should the prayers include certain words? Did he want them to sing during worship? If so, what should they sing? And who should decide? And who did God want to be their pastors and deacons? And how should a person become a member of a church — by birthright or by choice?

And what did God expect from members?

They weren't supposed to be asking these questions. The Church of England already had the answers. King James did not tolerate people who felt his church needed to be purified of false ceremonies, superstitious rituals, misleading interpretations, and other supposed remnants of papism. The congregational cell system did not succeed in protecting everyone from discovery. Preachers and writers — and not just Separatists — were hanged. Believers were imprisoned. Moses Fletcher was charged with attending the secret burial of a child, an attempt to avoid the ceremony of the Church of England. James Chilton's wife got in trouble for the same thing. Christopher Martin was cited for refusing to kneel at communion, then for refusing to follow Church of England ritual. Other Puritans and Separatists spent time in jail, in some cases the rest of their foreshortened lives. Prisoners often did not long survive the unsanitary filth of prisons and the rampant infections of overcrowding. Meals weren't part of the deal. Food had to be brought by outsiders and distributed by guards. A long prison sentence was often a death sentence.

Under these threatening circumstances, a minister in Babworth, Richard Clyfton, found himself evolving out of Church of England beliefs to the less ceremonious Puritan beliefs. From Puritanism he found himself wandering into the desperate realm of Separatism. His sermons were famous for contradicting the popish demands of the king's church. People in search of true worship — people *serious* about their relationship with God — came miles to hear him. Among his pious and curious congregation were William Brewster, of Scrooby, and a twelve-year old orphan named William Bradford. He had lost his father at the age of one and his mother at the age of seven, after which he was given to his grandfather, who died when the boy was twelve. And uncle then raised him and tried to turn him into a farmer, but he failed. The boy was weak and ill and far more inclined to read a book than shovel manure. His intense interest in the Bible and the meaning of the Scriptures led him as a young teen to Richard Clyfton's ministry. Hearing Clyfton, his thoughts turned radically liberal.

In 1604, King James tried to put a stop to the radical preachings of Puritans and Separatists. He demanded that all ministers conform to the Book of Common Prayer and the norms of the Church of England. Those who did not conform would be ousted from their churches. Clyfton and other "nonconformists" then had a decision to make: God or king.

Clyfton chose God. Ironically, doing so left him without a church, at least in the stone-and-mortar sense. But the Separatists offered another kind of church, one as separate from stone and mortar as it was from the earthly whims of a king. It existed where the faithful came together to worship in accordance with the word of God. One such place, just six or seven miles away, in the hamlet of Scrooby, was the home of William Brewster, his wife Mary, and their first two children. The Separatists of Scrooby needed a pastor. Clyfton needed a church and home. Brewster's place became both, and young Bradford became part of the congregation.

It was a bit run-down but otherwise a pretty nice place to live. It was owned by the Archibishopric and called the Manor House. It had known such visitors as King John in 1212, King Henry VII's daughter Margaret Tudor in 1503, Cardinal John Wolsey in 1530, and King Henry VIII in 1541. The people who assembled there to hear Richard Clyfton, however, were hardly of such royal stock. Rather, they were commoners with an uncommon need to make contact with God and to do God's will. Not the Pope's will. Not the king's will. *God's.*

Like Clyfton, Brewster had studied at Cambridge, a hothouse of Puritan thought. Cambridge students and professors were being arrested, imprisoned, tortured, and, in one case, strangled, and burned in a public execution. Brewster had good reason to toe the line of the Church of England, but his studies made him a thinking man. He worked under William Davison, a Puritan and British ambassador to

Netherlands, which was at the time was at war with Spain. During trips to Amsterdam and Leyden, Brewster witnessed the possibility of religious freedom.

In 1590, Brewster's father died. William inherited not only his property but his positions, including those of bailiff, innkeeper, and royal postmaster. He was short of aristocratic, but compared to the rest of Scrooby, he was someone to look up to. The Manor House was a six-acre compound with a moat on three sides and a river on the fourth. It had forty rooms and a chapel. It held the Brewsters. It held the Clyftons. And once or twice a week it held a secret congregation of scores of underground worshippers.

Some of those worshippers were following their beloved Richard Clyfton, walking several dangerous miles to hear him. One of them was the orphan Bradford, whose teenage curiosity was being stuffed with Clyfton's Separatist thoughts. Another member was John Robinson, who had been a Fellow at Cambridge, then parish minister of St. Andrew's Church in Norwich, then a former minister with big ideas and no church.

In other words, King James' crackdown was backfiring. His attempt to force the faithful to conform was only forcing them underground. Rather than conform, they separated, and deposed ministers such as Clyfton and Robinson became the sparks of new Separatist fires.

Separatism was by no means a mass movement or an organized rebellion. The groups were small and far between. Each Separatist church — and there were only a few — operated not only secretly but independently. They didn't belong to a broader group or report to a remote hierarchy. They named their own leaders. They openly discussed their beliefs and confessed their confusions.

They did so at night, with lamps low, curtains drawn, shutters closed. No sign out front said "Separatist Church." They arrived and left quietly, surreptitiously, in small groups, aware that men were watching their houses and inquiring about their comings and goings. They knew they had committed capital crimes. They'd listened to a minister who had neglected to wear a proper gown. They'd failed to kneel to pray, and they'd prayed their own prayers. They'd read the wrong Bible. For this, they knew, they would someday have to pay.

Psalm 1 said *Blessed [is] the man that walketh not in the counsel of the ungodly, nor standeth in the way of sinners, nor sitteth in the seat of the scornful,* but still, things were getting worse. More people were getting arrested, their property seized, their lives threatened. When Mrs. Brewster gave birth to her second daughter, they named her Fear.

By 1607, it was clear that the Scrooby group had to

leave England. They decided to move, en masse, to Holland, a country more liberal and socio-politically advanced than England. Though a small country, it produced half the books published in Europe. The University of Leyden was among the oldest universities in Europe. Holland's economy was already evolving beyond manufacturing in to the more sophisticated business of trading. The Dutch government tolerated any reasonably Christian religion. Holland looked like a good place for people who couldn't contain their thoughts.

King James, however, wanted errant thoughts contained. He allowed neither dissenters nor Catholics license to travel abroad. The Separatists had to bribe an English ship captain and pay an exorbitant fee to charter his ship to take them from Boston (a hundred miles north of London), south across the North Sea to Holland. Before the day of their escape, they quietly sold their houses, furniture, animals, and just about everything they couldn't carry. Under cover of darkness, a hundred and twenty-five desperate Christians sneaked down to the dock and rowed out to the ship with their worldly goods. But it wasn't just a ship. It was a trap. The captain had betrayed them. The ship's crew helped themselves to the Separatists' belongings until the sheriff's officers showed up. The officers hauled the Separatists back to the wharf, "rifled and ransacked them,"

William Bradford later wrote, "searched to their shirts for money, yea even the women, further than became modesty; and then carried them back into the town, and made them a spectacle and wonder to the multitude, which came flocking on all sides to behold them." They were stripped of their money, their books, everything of value. Clyfton, Robinson, Brewster and four others were thrown into two dark, filthy jail cells measuring just six feet by eight. The rest were ordered back to Scrooby. Following their trials, the jailed leaders were condemned to prison for a month.

Now refugees in their own town, the destitute Separatists had to beg for living space and food. They spent the winter there, living off the mercy of friends and family, no doubt to the angst and irritation of all.

With no jobs or homes to hold them, their benefactors surely eager to be free of them, their king hardly inclined to loosen his holy rule, the Separatists still had every reason to flee the country. Come the spring of 1608, they had to try again.

This time they hired a Dutch captain and devised a scheme to meet his ship at an isolated stretch of beach at the mouth of the Humber River, some forty miles north of Boston. For seventy-five or a hundred people to parade down the road to a remote beach would be too obvious. They had to split up. The men would walk in small groups.

The women and children would load themselves and their bundles of goods onto a barge with Clyfton, Robinson, and Brewster. Under cover of darkness, the barge would sneak down estuaries and tributaries until it reached the rendez-vous.

The ship arrived but the tide went out, stranding the barge in a mud bank somewhere in the dark. The men wait-ed anxiously until the captain sent a longboat to get them. The tide wouldn't be in until well after daylight, so the men thought it best to move out to the ship. Some were on board, others still awaiting their ride, when the king's soldiers ar-rived, armed with guns and other weapons, some on horse-back, others on foot. The men on the ship could only watch as the soldiers arrested their friends on the beach. The cap-tain, himself in big trouble if he got caught, weighed an-chor and headed for Holland. When the barge arrived, the women, children, and leaders were also arrested, though in the dark and confusion a few managed to escape.

It's hard to say who had worse luck — those on the ship or those left behind. The ship hit a storm that blew them nearly to the coast of Norway. For fourteen days waves pounded the boat until it nearly filled with water. It surely would have foundered had the application of intense prayer not succeeded where bailing had failed. They arrived in Holland but without their wives, children, friends, leaders, possessions, or any idea what had happened as they sailed away.

Back in England, the people under arrest suffered a similar storm, but one of courts rather than weather. Judges and magistrates passed them around — women weeping, children clinging to them, all of them destitute, homeless, hungry, and cold. Prison didn't seem fair because innocent children would be separated from their mothers, and the mothers had only been following their husbands. Fines wouldn't work because they had no money. After much misery, pleading and public wailing, the easiest solution was to just let them go, or at least disappear. Little by little, they made their way to Holland. Clyfton, Robinson, and Brewster were the last to go.

Once in Holland the Separatists took up residence in Amsterdam, then moved to Leyden a year later. In Holland they worshipped as they reckoned God wanted them to worship. Nobody stood between them and God; nobody told them what to believe, when to kneel, or how to worship. But Dutch liberalism turned out to have its drawbacks. Toleration, it turned out, provided protection not just for Separatists but for Jews, Turks, Arminians, Catholics, Anabaptists, and any other misguided group that felt like opening up a church founded on dubious interpretation of scripture. The Separatists knew enough to suspect and avoid such churches. The warning appeared clearly in Corinthians, that people would come preaching in the name of Jesus but would do so with lies.

Miscreant churches weren't the only problem. Separatist children were easing into the Dutch community, where "evill examples" tempted them into "extravagance." As the expiration of a Dutch-Spanish armistice approached, the army tempted young men to the patently unchristian profession of soldiering. Protestants worried that a renewal of the Spanish Inquisition might reach Holland. It was not an unreasonable fear. Spain had controlled Spanish Netherlands — the areas now known as Belgium, Luxembourg, and a northern area of France — since 1579. Many of the English remembered Spain's Invincible Armada. Just twenty years earlier it had tried to invade England. Spain was not a distant threat.

Meanwhile, religion aside, the Dutch economy had stagnated, and the Separatists were low-skill laborers in a relatively high-tech country. Hard work earned wages barely sufficient for survival. They didn't see themselves getting ahead in life. After twelve years, they began to regret their move to Holland.

Then, in what was becoming a Separatist tradition, things went from bad to worse. William Brewster's press published a book titled *Perth Assembly,* about King James' questionable religious policies in Scotland. The books made their way to England and, inevitably to the king. Irritated yet again by separatist thought, he directed his ambassador in Holland to demand that the press be destroyed, its operator, William Brewster, arrested and extradited. The Dutch government, needing to keep England as an ally against Spain, cooperated. Authorities seized Brewster's press, but they couldn't find Brewster. He was in England. He now had warrants out for his arrest in two countries. Holland was no longer far enough from the Church of England — across the southern corner of the North Sea, yes, but apparently not far enough for survival. If the Separatists really wanted to separate, they needed more than a corner of a sea between them and the king; they needed an ocean.

Chapter One

The Deal

The Separatists began to think about the New World. Bradford wrote of their discussions:

> *The place they had thoughts on was some of those vast and unpeopled countries of America, which are reported to be fruitful and fit for habitation, being devoid of all civil inhabitants, where there are only savage and brutish men, which range up and down little otherwise than the wild beasts of the same.*

The idea generated debates of fear and temptation — the fear of savages, beasts, famine, misery, the temptations of freedom and the good, clean, Godly, Separatist way of life. They finally decided that an invasion of Holland by Spain might prove Spanish Catholics more vicious than American savages, that King James's officers had already proven more brutal than beasts, and that famine and misery pretty much described the situation in Leyden, not to mention the average English prison. How much worse could the New World be?

They debated where to go. The information they had to work with was based on rumor and the boosterism of explorers looking for settlers. They considered Guiana, on the northeast corner of South America. It was a country "rich, fruitful, and blessed with a perpetual spring and a flourishing greenness," William Bradford wrote, "where vigorous nature brought forth all things in abundance and plenty without any great labor or art of man. But there were arguments to the contrary. Such countries are subject to grievous diseases and many noisome impediments which other more temperate places are freer from, and would not so well agree with our English bodies." And besides, if they went there and did well, the Spaniard would just come in and "displant or overthrow them, as he did the French in Florida."

They considered the Dutch territory along the Hudson River. The Dutch West India Company was looking for people to colonize the area. But no, the Separatists had pretty much had it with the Dutch, and they didn't want to *be* Dutch. Despite their years in Holland, they were English.

The land the English claimed in North America, essentially all of the eastern seaboard, from Florida to Maine, was called Virginia. Captain John Smith's descriptions of southern Virginia looked pretty good. The coast had already been explored and a few maps were available. The Virginia Company was advertising the good life to be had in its temperate territory. Anyone who wanted to settle there would be given a patent, i.e. permission, to do so.

But no, southern Virginia, too, had its problems. For one thing, the settlement at Jamestown already had a reputation for lethargy, loose morals, and political confusion. For another, Jamestown had Indian problems, including skirmishes, raids, sieges, theft, torture and executions, all carried out by English as well as Powhatans. Things were not going well at all. If the Separatists knew much about the short history of colonial Virginia — and we don't know whether they did — they'd surely see a potential parallel between Jamestown and the ghost-colony of Roanoke. Almost a hundred men, women and children had moved to Roanoke from England. Not long after their arrival, they disappeared without a trace.

But the big problem with Jamestown wasn't its neighbors. It was, in a sense, its name. The Separatists knew better than to flee to a place named after the king they were fleeing. Jamestown was firmly in the fold of the Church of England. Settling too close would mean risk of persecution, yet settling too far away would mean no help in case of attack by the Spanish, the French, or the Americans.

Tough decision. The Separatists of Leyden fasted to clear their minds for God's message. God advised them to hedge their bet. They should settle under the wing of the Virginia Company but as far as possible from Jamestown. If they left in early spring, they would have time to build houses before winter, salt away some fish, get the lay of the land, maybe even plant and harvest a little something for the cold months.

In 1617, the congregation sent John Carver and Robert Cushman to London to negotiate an agreement. They needed the king's permission and the Virginia Company's support. Without sounding like they had anything radically anti-Church-of-England in mind, they had to find out how much religious leeway the king and his church would allow them. The question itself might have led to arrest on the spot or a prohibition against any settlement or business in Virginia. Carver and Cushman didn't dare do the asking themselves. They let a couple of Virginia Company officers, Separatist sympathizers, approach the king and church authorities. They downplayed the religious aspect of the venture, emphasized the development, the growth, the exports — in short, the money. The king asked how these people would earn their living. Told that they would be fishermen, he is said to have exclaimed, "So God have my soul, 'tis an honest trade. 'twas the apostles' own calling."

It wasn't exactly a yes or a no, but it sounded pretty good. James couldn't just declare Separatism acceptable. But accept its wayward tendencies he might, albeit for reasons more economic than religious. He wanted a stronger foothold in the New World. The country's best timber had already been turned into ships, furniture, and firewood. The fishing grounds around England still had plenty of herring, but the good cod was off the coast of North America. The Spanish, French, Portuguese, and Dutch already had colonies and trading posts up and down both coasts of the Americas. Sugar and rosewood were coming in from Brazil, gold and silver from Peru and Mexico, cod from Newfoundland, pelts from Maine. England's stake in the New World consisted of not much more than a struggling little settlement at Jamestown and some optimistic maps that showed a string of places with English names but no English people.

King James wanted to put people there. It would be even better if that emigration conveniently cleansed England of religious dissidents without the political mess caused by extermination. It would be even better if they were families that would reproduce and spread into new territories. Without exactly forgiving the Separatists for their crimes, without even recognizing their religion, King James quietly granted permission for the group to settle in Virginia.

By then, however, the Virginia Company was suffering financial difficulties. It no longer offered to underwrite new settlements. It would issue patents only to groups with independent financial support. With the people back in Leyden antsy to get going, Carver and Cushman negotiated with a London-based wheeler-dealer named Thomas Weston. He was somewhat sympathetic with Puritanism. He was even more sympathetic with his own self-interest. Hoping to satisfy both sympathies, he rounded up investors for a longshot scheme. Just by moving to Virginia and promising to work for seven years, they could buy into a transatlantic joint-stock venture that might well yield a fortune impossible to earn in England. Their sweat-equity would equal a ten-pound investment, one share in the venture without actually paying anything. And for anybody who had a little capital to invest, ten pounds would get them an additional share.

Investors recognized the risk but liked the payoff. Investment in the New World was an investment in timber, fish, crops, furs, tobacco, maybe even gold. If it worked out, it would sure beat investment in an antiquated textile mill.

England was losing its lead in that industry. Other countries were learning to use water to drive looms, and they could produce better cloth at lower prices. English investors were looking for somewhere else to put their money. America looked like the right place.

America was also the only place a peasant or worker could hope to own a piece of land. In England, the landed gentry were either born into land or by some miracle given a piece of it by the king. In America, one could work out an agreement with the Virginia Company and within a few years of indentured work join the ranks of landowners. The American dream was, first, an English dream.

Weston orchestrated two groups: the investors who would remain in London, known as "Adventurers," and the emigrants, known as "Planters." The Adventurers and Planters drew up a ten-point agreement. Adventurers could buy as many shares as they could afford. Each Planter over the age of sixteen would receive a share. If they provided their own provision, they'd receive an additional share. Two Planters between the ages of ten and sixteen would equal one adult, together worth one share.

Ten pounds in 1620 was a tidy pile of money. By certain economic measurements, ten pounds in 1620 had the purchasing power that 1,278 pounds, 2,259 U.S. dollars, or 1,881 euros would have in 2002. The conversion means little, however, due to the entirely different lifestyles and economics of the seventeenth and twenty-first centuries. Ten pounds in 1620 in England exceeded the amount a laborer might earn in a year, but $2,259 in 2002 in the United States would not sustain human life. A few could afford to invest in extra shares, Christopher Martin, John Carver, and William Mullins among them. (For whatever it's worth, in 2004 a top-deck "Superior Balcony" cabin on the Jewel of the Seas, London to Boston, one-way, leaving in September, cost $2,213, including tax and insurance.)

Under Weston's plan, the money thus raised would be used for ships, equipment, and provisions. The Planters would work for seven years, building houses, tilling the ground, planting crops, and "making such commodities as shall be useful for the colony." They'd work four days for the venture, leaving two days for their own projects, and one, of course, for the worship of God. For the venture they'd catch fish and send it back salted. They'd cut oak, maple, and walnut, and send it back all sawed up. They'd barter with wild savages, trading trinkets for beaver, otter and marten pelts. They'd dig up aromatic roots of sassafras and send them back. The Adventurers back in London would sell these commodities and keep track of the revenues. At the end of seven years, the chattel and total revenues would be divided among Adventurers and Planters in accordance

with their shares. The Planters would then be free of all debt
and obligation, and they could keep the houses they had
built and the land they had cleared and tilled. Seven years
of labor and danger would earn them more than they'd earn
in a lifetime in England or Holland. And even as they grew
rich, they'd be avoiding an eternity in Hell. Making money,
avoiding papal blasphemy *and* lining themselves up on the
right side of God — it looked like a pretty good deal.

The venture, then, had characteristics of capitalism and
cooperativism, revenue and religion, business and family,
real estate and redemption. Profit, pure, simple, and beautiful, was the express purpose of the venture, an impetus
that has always motivated human projects as surely as, if
ever so differently than, religion. Much of the profit would
go to people who had contributed no direct labor. The community of Planters as a whole held responsibility for the
obligation, and the goods they took to America were essentially owned in common. They'd work together to build
each family a house, though all the houses would be owned
in common until the great liquidation seven years hence.
All the Planters had to work, and the fruit of their collective
labor would be divided among all investors. The Planters
didn't especially like the part about the whole community
being responsible for the obligation to the Adventurers,
but the Separatists were desperate to get out of Holland, to

leave England and Europe behind, and to get closer to their God before the world came to an end.

Once they had their finances lined up, they devised their final plan. They would buy one ship and charter another. The best ship they could afford to buy was a used sixty-ton freighter called the *Speedwell.* She wasn't really designed for oceanic voyages, but the price was right. She was a little on the small side, but if fitted with a taller mast and wider spars, she looked like she could make it across the ocean. Smaller ships had done it. She would stay with the Planters for use as a fishing and trading vessel. The other ship, the chartered one, would sail to Virginia, unload its passengers and supplies, then sail back to England, ideally with the first load of commodities. These products would finance more supplies and another ship to Virginia. It was a good plan. What could possibly go wrong?

Actually, a lot of things could go wrong, among them French pirates, Spanish conquistadors, local savages, internal uprisings, bad weather, even wild animals. The Separatists had little if any experience in killing wild animals, let alone people. In that military service was compulsory for English men between the ages of sixteen and sixty, some of the Planters probably had a little experience with weaponry. But they weren't officers or professional soldiers. To survive on a continent they envisioned as unsettled by anyone but brutish savages and still contested by equally brutish European explorers and exploiters, they needed a little military support — not necessarily a garrison of protectors but at least an advisor who knew something of weaponry and tactics.

They had two candidates: John Smith, who had founded the colony at Jamestown, and Myles Standish, an English military man who happened to be in Holland and in need of a job.

John Smith would seem the stronger of the candidates. He had solid experience in starting a colony on a new continent. Granted, Jamestown hadn't developed as smoothly or profitably as hoped. Relationships with the local natives were horrifically violent, and settlers were dying of disease, wounds, or starvation just about as fast as they arrived. Only with politically complex contortions of carrots, sticks, and alliances was the colony able to trade trinkets for desperately needed food. The immigrant Christians applied threats, revenge, and torture to uncooperative tribes, but the local animists proved equally capable of crossing trade with terrorism. Hundreds of English colonists died of hunger and wounds before the Powhatan princess Pocahontas married a young colonist, John Rolfe, in 1614, effecting a few years of peace. Two years later, Rolfe took her to London, where the air pollution bothered with her until she died of a lung ailment. She was a celebrity, and the Separatists may have known the whole story.

The Virginia Company had recalled Smith after some serious political bickering that ended with gunpowder exploding against his thighs and torso, burning him badly. He returned to England in considerable pain but sailed back to North America in 1614 to look for other places to live. He had maps of the coast and plenty of advice on where best to settle. Prince Charles, young son of James, had the privilege of naming the bays, rivers, capes, and other features of the coast of New England, among them the Charles River, Cape Ann, Massachusetts, and a nice little harbor that looked to him like a place that should be called Plymouth. A lot of this information had already appeared in a book that Smith had written, *A Description of New England*, published in 1616. The Separatists apparently had the book and the map, and thus felt they had little need of Smith himself, especially considering how much he wanted to be paid.

To a group of colonial hopefuls on a shoestring budget, Myles Standish was the better deal. He had military experience, and apparently his financial requirements implied that personal enrichment wasn't his top priority. Even though he wasn't of their church, they liked him. He was a little on the short side, perhaps a bit quick to lose his temper, but there was something about him they liked. Maybe he was a little less brash and blustery than Smith, less of a real estate booster. Maybe he seemed interested more in the adventure than the money. Maybe it was because he wanted to take his wife. After all, as far as the Separatists were concerned, this wasn't really a business venture. It was a family plan. They were going to America to live.

Chapter Two

The *Mayflower*

The *Speedwell* left the port of Delftshaven, Holland, in July of 1620 for the short trip through the Straits of Dover and down the English Channel to Southampton. A man named Reynolds served as her master. Among the thirty or so Separatist passengers on board were activist William Bradford, church elder William Brewster, John Carver, Edward Winslow, deacon Samuel Fuller, and John Howland. Pastor John Robinson stayed in Leyden with the rest of the congregation. Their plan was to come to the colony later, as soon as the first party had established the basic comforts.

At about the time the *Speedwell* left Leyden, a chartered ship named *Mayflower* sailed out of London for Southampton. She may have carried as many as ninety passengers. A few may have been committed Puritans or Separatists, a few others may have leaned in that direction, and the rest were apparently not bothered by the prospect of a long trip in close quarters with people who took their religion very seriously. None considered themselves committed cargo, but cargo they were, packed into the gun deck of a high-pooped, pot-bellied merchantman.

No designs, drawings, or descriptions of the *Mayflower* have survived to modern times. Historians can only conjecture the probable specifications of a hundred-and-eighty-ton high-pooped pot-bellied merchantman. The high poop was a two-story housing at the stern. The potbelly was her midship bulge. Her widest point was probably some twenty-six feet on a sixty-four-foot keel. She bulged widest just a foot and a half above the waterline. Though the midriff bulge may have looked a little like a rim of fat squeezed up over a belt, the extra flotation at water level smoothed and minimized her rocking in moderate seas. At the level of the upper deck, she was only about nineteen feet wide. Loaded, she drew twelve feet of water at her deepest point, the stern end of her keel. She measured close to 113 feet from stem to stern. Because the forward part of the hull was relatively flat, she didn't exactly slice through water; she tended to slide up over it, a soft and gentle lurching. She sailed well with a good wind behind her but bucked a bit if struggling against wind or current. Depending on the route Master Jones took, the *Mayflower* may have sailed west against the Westerlies and south against the Gulf Stream, softly lurching toward the New World.

As a 180-ton ship, the *Mayflower* could carry 180 barrels, called "tuns," each of which, filled with 252 gallons of beer, water or wine, would weigh about a ton. That many tuns might not actually fit into the hold, but if by some miracle of malleable barrels they were somehow tucked in, she'd be carrying about 180 tons.

We have no pictures or designs of the *Mayflower*, but historians are pretty sure what she looked like. Her masts were probably of pine, spruce, or fir, quite possibly from Norway, but they may have been of oak. She had three masts: the mizzenmast, which rose just forward of the poophouse at the stern; the mainmast, which stood just aft of the hatch at the center of the ship; and the foremast, which rose from the forecastle deck near the bow. The sails draped from these masts could catch something like 525 square yards of wind.

The main shaft of the mainmast rose some forty feet from the upper deck to the mainyard, the cross-piece from which the mainsail hung. The mainyard was fifty feet across, almost twice the width of the hull. A twenty-four-foot topmast stood atop the mainmast. The topmast held the main topsail yard, the cross-piece from which the main topsail hung. The topsail yard reached about half as wide as the mainyard below it. The sail it held was about twenty feet wide at the top, forty-five feet wide at the bottom. Above the topmast stood a fourteen-foot staff that held aloft the King's Colors, the flag that announced that the *Mayflower* was a merchantman, not a pirate ship nor a military vessel. The mainmast tilted back about one foot for each thirty feet of height.

The foremast, up at the bow, rose thirty feet above the forecastle deck and held a nineteen-foot topmast with a ten-foot flagstaff. The flagstaff probably bore either of two controversial flags. One was of the country's older flag, the red cross on white background, the cross of St. George, patron saint of England. The country's newer flag, the one made official by King James in 1606, showed two crosses: that of St. George, and the white cross of St. Andrew, patron saint of Scotland. (Together, on the Scottish blue background, they looked like the modern Union Jack, which bears an additional red cross, that of Ireland's St. Patrick laid diagonally across the flag.) Many people refused to fly the new flag. The English didn't like the blue background that obscured their original white background. The Scots didn't like St. George's red cross laid atop St. Andrew's white cross. Many people didn't like the implications of equality represented by both crosses on the same flag. Which way the *Mayflower* leaned, no one knows.

The mizzenmast, at the stern, rose some thirty-two feet above the half deck with an eight-foot pennant staff atop. The mizzenmast held a forty-two-foot yard that rose diagonally at an angle of about forty-five degrees. The triangular sail it held, called a lateen, was therefore high at one end, low at the other. It pivoted around the mizzen to catch the wind on one side or the other, helping to steer the ship.

The masts and yards may have been of light-weight evergreen, but the rest of the ship was solid English oak — wood strong enough to take a battering at sea and heavy enough to keep the sails, masts and yards from tipping her over in a high wind.

People and cargo descended into the ship through the main hatch at the center of the deck, just forward of the mainmast. About eight feet wide and nineteen feet long, the hatch was covered with a lattice during good weather, ventilating the gun deck where the passengers lived. There were probably two other smaller hatches, one fore, one aft. During bad weather, caps fit over the hatches to keep water out. With no windows or lamps — flames would have to be extinguished during rough weather — the passengers would have to ride out the storm in near darkness.

41

Most or all of the crew slept in the forecastle (pronounced by sailors, and often spelled, "fo'c'sle"), a little "castle" at the fore end of the main deck. There the crew may have slept in the latest of bed technology, the hammock that Christopher Colombus had brought back from the Caribbean along with the semblence of a Taino Indian word that sounded like *hamaca*. The forecastle also housed the galley, a single wood stove made of brick under a large copper bowl. Here all food for crew and passengers was prepared. In the event of rough seas, the cook shut down the fire lest the tossing of the ship cause an ember to set their little world afire. The ship carried no other fire except for the small flames of lamps, which were enclosed in horn and never left unattended. Passengers may have burned bits of wood in small stoves to heat food for individual families.

The helmsman steered the ship from the level of the main deck by maneuvering a whipstaff, a vertical shaft attached to the tiller down below at aft of the gun deck. The tiller turned the rudder left and right. Standing at deck level inside the poop, the helmsman could not see the world through which he was sailing. He had walls to his sides. Ahead, he saw little more than the lower end of the mast, the bottom of the mainsail, and the forecastle up at the bow. He had a compass, but if not well out to sea, he needed an officer on the deck above him to shout down orders to turn.

A small hatch allowed the voice to travel down to him.

Master Jones had two officers reporting to him. The first mate, John Clark, served as pilot who would guide the ship when it was near shore. Clark had already sailed to Virginia and New England several times. In 1611, a Spanish caravel captured him in Virginia, took him to Havana, then to Spain. He was released in 1616 in a prisoner exchange. He'd been to Virginia as recently as 1619. He was about forty years old when he signed onto the *Mayflower*.

The second mate, Robert Coppin, was also a pilot. He had been to New England at least once before and was hired for his knowledge of the coastline. Little is known of him. As second mate, he probably may have had the only private cabin, the upper story of the poop, which rode high at the stern. Though he had the most privacy, he also had the most exciting ride. When the ship rocked in the waves, sometimes an arc of almost ninety degrees, the people farthest from the waterline traveled the farthest distance. The second mate's bunk might arc ten feet or more. A man high on the main topmast might swing a stomach-flipping thirty or forty feet in a few seconds.

If the second mate had the upper story of the poop, the first mate shared Master Jones's cabin at the level of the main deck. The captain sacrificed privacy for the convenience and efficiency of having a navigator close at hand.

It's also possible that Clark and Coppin shared the upper cabin of the poop.

There may also have been a third mate aboard. If there were three officers, two of them probably shared a bunk, taking turns during their alternating shifts. One mate was always awake and on duty. He had to advise the helmsman which way to steer. He also had to keep track of the constant measurements needed to navigate across an ocean without markers or milestones.

The ship also had a surgeon, Giles Heale. Little is known of him except that he would survive the round trip to America and later take up practice in London. He was on board for the many problems that can befall a sailor: mangled fingers from rigging and pulleys, broken bones from falls, gangrene from slight injuries, internal ailments from unsanitary conditions, pulmonary infections from the cold and wet, bullets from pirate ships, splinters from cannonballs ripping through the hull. Indeed the cures themselves, involving the letting of blood, the drilling of skulls, the application of mercury and lead, and doses of anything from horse, hare and hen dung to crab juice beyond its prime gave the surgeon a slim margin of success.

As a surgeon, Mr. Heale probably had been an apprentice in a hospital but hadn't studied at a university. (Thus he was Mister, not Doctor, Heale.) He was licensed in 1619 by the Company of Barber-Surgeons. As a barber, he could not only cut hair but treat external wounds and draw blood. As a surgeon, he could treat internal wounds. He probably did the work of a physician, too, dispensing medicine for internal ailments. If he received his license in 1619, he was probably rather young when the *Mayflower* set out in 1620. He couldn't have had much experience. As conditions on a ship differed from those in a hospital, he probably had to learn as he went along. He was probably smart enough to include in his medicine chest a copy of *The Surgeon's Mate*, by John Woodall, first published in 1617. As surgeon-general for the East India Company, Woodall had developed practices, procedures and medical kits appropriate for long voyages. A medical chest to Woodall's recommendations would include an incision knife, a dismembering knife, a mallet and chisel for amputating fingers, cauterizing irons for searing veins and arteries shut, a terebellum for removing bullets, a crows-bill forceps, storks-bill forceps, goose-bill forceps, a speculum oris with a screw for opening body orifices, dental forceps of various grades of steel for the removal of teeth of various hardnesses (softer steel being less likely to shatter a fragile tooth), a head saw, a spare saw blade, a crown saw with a T-shaped handle for drilling an inch-wide hole in the skull, a lenticulur for trimming around the hole in the skull, a forceps for removing bone

45

fragments from the surface of the brain, a probe forceps for reaching into the brain, a steel catheter, an enema syringe, an ear-picker, and a paring knife. Woodall knew that acidic fruits, such as lemons and limes, would prevent scurvy. He prescribed cloves for the heart, brain, liver, stomach, eyes, problems with digestion, bad breath, and inadequate "lust," which in the language of the day referred to strength and vitality, a diagnosis that might be known in post-Freudian days as depression. He recommended bathing gout with a mixture of salt boiled in wine.

Mr. Heale treated the crew. The Separatist deacon Samuel Fuller treated the passengers. We do not know whether they shared information, medicines and instruments. We don't know which of them knew more or which thought he knew more. But most likely Heale had had more training than Fuller, who probably took on the job of healing because the physical wellbeing of the flock came with the title of deacon.

The passengers lived on the gun deck, also called the 'tween deck because it was between the main deck and the hold. Here a hundred and two passengers, and maybe some crewmembers, shared a space of about 1,800 square feet. If the gun deck had held nothing but a hundred and two people, they would have had an average of about eighteen square feet each, not much more than the space of a single bed. Some families may have built bunk beds, thus opening up a little more space, but quarters were still very tight. In their midst was the carry-on baggage that everyone would need during a two-month voyage. It is almost certain that assorted goats, chickens, and pigs took up space, too. (There's no real evidence that they took any animals at all, but it's logical that they did.) They wouldn't have taken sheep, horses or cows not only for lack of space for the animals and their food but because once in America, such large grazing animals would need clear pastures, the last thing these people expected to find in the North American wilderness.

The gun deck also carried other equipment the crew needed for the trip. When the crew had to turn the capstan — a stout, vertical shaft that winched sails up and down and hoisted cargo through the hatch — passengers had to clear a ten-foot circle around it. The crew also needed aisles cleared among the passengers and their clutter. The gun deck also held the disassembled sections of a shallop, a boat about thirty feet long and ten feet wide that could hold sixteen men and could be sailed under its single mast or rowed. As people expanded into every available space, some came to inhabit the cradling curves of the shallop. In the end, each person had less than the space of a single bed. They had to ride scrunched up, elbow-to-elbow, draped over each other, in physical contact with other people almost constantly.

The passengers also shared the gun deck with a few guns —at least four medium-sized cannons, called minions, and a number of sakers. The minions were brass cannons of 800 to 1,200 pounds and a bore of about 2.9 inches. They could shoot a three-and-a-half-pound ball some 1,600 yards. Sakers were a little smaller, weighing 650 to 800 pounds. With a bore of about 2.7 inches, it could shoot a two-and-three-quarters-pound ball 1,700 yards — almost a mile. Sakers and minions were mounted on bases with wheels that allowed them to be pulled back from the gun port for reloading.

If pirates came alongside — not an unlikely event — the cannons would be rolled to the four gun ports on that side of the ship. These small, rectangular holes were sealed shut with wooden covers and pine pitch to keep water out. The gunners would yank the covers open only when the ship was threatened with something worse than high seas. The ship most likely carried two cannons at the stern, a pirate's most likely point of approach simply because the *Mayflower* would be running away. It would take an attacker a few hours to catch up, at best making three miles an hour to the cargo ship's one or two, depending on the weather. During that slow chase, the cannons could hurl four-pound shot at their pursuer in hopes of hitting some tender and crucial spot. They would have been shooting into the wind, of course, so their range would be cut short a bit. Given the movement of the ship and the general inaccuracy of these cannon, they probably wouldn't hit much from just a few hundred yards away.

The ship probably had a few murderers on deck. These breech-loaded, swivel-mounted four-and-a-half-foot guns were well named. Their bores were a little more than an inch in diameter, wider at the muzzle than at the breech. Loaded with several pieces of iron and stone, they could spray an attacking ship as it came close, potentially killing several attackers with a single shot.

The *Mayflower* would have offered pathetic resistance to any serious attack, but at the same time, the prize to the attacker would have been pretty pathetic, too. No gold, silver or doubloons. No furs or fish. Just a lot of wet people, their pathetic possessions, their one big desperate dream, and maybe a dozen used cannons, still warm.

We do not know the origin of the *Mayflower*, who built her or where her keel was laid. *Mayflower* was a fairly common name for ships of that time, but we don't even know what kind of flower the name referred to. It may have been the lily-of-the-valley, the hawthorn, or the cowslip. The

Oxford English Dictionary says it could be any of several flowers that bloom in May. The *Mayflower* may have been the Tudor rose, named after the royal family that ruled from Henry VII until the passing of Elizabeth. At any rate, the name apparently didn't mean much to its passengers. Nothing they wrote — at least nothing that survives — refers to her by name. The word "May-flower" appears on a 1623 land record, but other than that, all writings refer to her as simply *the ship.*

The commonness of the name makes it hard to identify which *Mayflower* made the historic voyage to America. The first reference we have to the *Mayflower* of the Pilgrims dates from 1609. In that year, an Andrew Pawling hired her to go to Norway to pick up a load of herring, pine planks, and barrels of pine tar. Pawling needed these products most urgently. His debtors were after him, and the last of his assets were on a high-pooped, pot-bellied merchantman sailing the notoriously violent North Sea. The weather turned against him as a storm kept the ship at sea for several weeks. To stay afloat, Master Christopher Jones, the captain and part owner of the ship, had to heave a good amount of Pawling's products into the bounding main. The *Mayflower* reached London to find Pawling in debtors prison and in no mood to learn that much of his hope was floating somewhere between Scotland and Norway. The value of the surviving products wasn't enough to bail him out.

Master Jones and the *Mayflower* spent the next ten years hauling English furs, iron, taffeta, hops, salt, tobacco and pewter goods to France, Spain, Norway and Germany, returning with wine and textiles. The *Mayflower's* hold smelled of fish, wine, turpentine, and tar. We have no record explaining why Master Jones decided to accept an assignment to carry passengers on a one-way trip across the Atlantic. He may have had a middle-age urge for adventure, the challenge of the open sea, and a glimpse of the other side of the world. He was about fifty years old and may have seen himself as having few years left for adventurous voyages. He saw money in it, too, and no doubt worked out a deal that would compensate him for his risk. His contract probably called for demurrage payments if the ship had to remain anchored in America for long.

In May 1620, Master Jones unloaded a cargo of wine from La Rochelle, France, and in July sailed south out of London, bound for Southampton with his cargo of Planters. There the *Mayflower* met the *Speedwell* and its cargo of Christians, just in from Holland.

Chapter Three

Problems at Port

When the *Mayflower* and *Speedwell* met at Southampton, the passengers no doubt hoped to hit the waves immediately. Spring had come and gone, summer had arrived, June had become July, and now they saw August just days away. Any possibility of planting that year had passed. Now, at best, they might hope to have houses built, a supply of fish salted away, a pile of firewood cut, stacked and split before winter set in. But to get anything done before the ground froze, they'd have to leave *right now*.

But they couldn't. To their dismay, financial problems and legal questions continued to delay the launch. With everybody dying to get going, Robert Cushman allowed that he had modified the deal with the Adventurers. The Planters wouldn't be working four days for the venture and two for themselves, with the seventh day reserved for the adoration of God. Under the secretly modified agreement, the Planters would give six days of labor to the venture each week. That labor would include, of course, the building of houses for the Planters, the tilling of their fields, and the harvesting of their crops. The housing and sustenance of themselves was part of their job, their obligation. They owed it to the venture.

Or so said Cushman. The actual modified Articles of Agreement, as he had them written down, left the workweek in the fog of good intentions. Article Three said, ...*all profits and benefits that are got, by trade, traffic, trucking, working, fishing, or any other means, of any person or persons, shall remain in the common stock until the division.* Article Five said, *That at the end of the seven years, the capital and profits, viz., the houses, land, goods and chattels, be equally divided among the Adventurers and Planters. . .*

In other words, whatever the Planters built, dug, sawed, split, planted, plowed, harvested, shot, caught, wrought, skinned, salted, staked out, hammered up, nailed down, whittled, weaved, received, discovered or devised would belong to everyone, Planters and Adventurers alike, in accordance with their shares. How much a given individual worked or produced had little to do with how much that person would own. And it didn't matter what day they did it on, what time of night, or on what holiday. If they made it, it belonged to the venture. They'd agreed to that, of course, except for the part about the houses belonging to the venture and the lack of time to pursue their own interests.

This was old-fashioned capitalism at its best, the investors doing nothing, demanding everything, and the workers giving literally one hundred percent to their jobs. Though they could build their own houses and produce their own food on company time, they wouldn't really own anything but a portion of this stuff. What percent of this stuff the Planters themselves could keep — that is, what percent of the venture they owned — is not known. Nor is it known, nor was it known at the time, whether their profits after seven years would be enough for them to buy the houses they had built and the land they had cleared, tilled, and defended. It would depend on how successful they were.

Before anyone sailed anywhere, someone had some explaining to do. The paper Mr. Cushman held in Southampton wasn't the one the Separatists had signed in Leyden. Now, despite the delay it would cause, the Planters fired off a letter to the investors. They didn't like these new terms and had never agreed to them. They hinted that they'd gladly abandon the venture except that they'd already sold everything they owned. They pointed out that they lacked many necessities, had "no oil, not a sole to mend a shoe, nor every man a sword to his side, wanting many muskets, much armour, etc." Despite the promise that the venture provide them with everything they needed, they already lacked provisions, and they hadn't even left port yet.

Despite the unapproved changes to the contract and the paucity of the promised supplies, the Planters strove for fairness. They added an extra article to the agreement and promised to work more than originally required. If seven years of labor failed to produce "large profits," they'd work more years. But they wanted two days for themselves and one day for God. Their houses would remain their houses, and their gardens would not be divided.

It still wasn't much of a contract. With such vague stipulations, it wasn't clear who was obliged to do what or how much profit would constitute "large." The contract probably wouldn't have held up in court, and even if it had, a good number of the signers might well have starved to death, or even died of old age, before a court reached a decision on a transatlantic case. In fact, a court may well have wondered what to do about a contract that had no signers. The Planters never signed the modified agreement that the Adventurers sent to them, and the Adventurers never signed the re-modified agreement that the Planters sent back. It was time to sail, and the agreement — the purported purpose of the whole trip — was of secondary interest.

As for the shortage of supplies, the passengers looked to Christopher Martin, governor of the *Mayflower*, representative of the non-Separatists who had come from London. He'd spent 700 pounds on provisions in Southampton. This is the same Christopher Martin who, many years earlier, had been arrested for refusing to kneel during communion. He wouldn't kneel to church authorities any more than he'd bow to the demands of his fellow passengers. Miffed that anyone had the audacity to question his efforts and integrity, Martin refused to give an accounting of the 700 pounds he'd spent. During the early negotiations with the Adventurers, he had represented the London contingent while Cushman had represented the Leyden contingent, the Separatists. Martin didn't especially like the Separatists. He called them "waspish, discontented people." And he probably didn't have much good to say about anyone else. He held himself in very high regard and looked down on the rest of the world, especially the unwashed peasantry who would accompany him to America. He had invested more than most or all of the Planters. Maybe this gave him a feeling of superiority. Cushman didn't think so. He considered Martin's contribution a little insignificant for a man of his means. Martin didn't agree and didn't care. He'd spent the 700 pounds, and the supplies were in the hold. End of question.

Not much could be done about Martin. The money was gone, the summer fading fast. As for the hundred-pound debt, the passengers, eager to get underway, sold sixty or eighty firkins of butter — 3360 to 4720 pounds — to pay off 60 pounds of the debt. They could live without butter. They just wanted to get going. They'd been working toward this moment for over three years. They were ready.

Chapter Four

More Problems

Finally, at last, on August 5, all cargo and passengers on board, the rigging rigged, the sails unfurled, fear, frustration, impatience, and hope in everyone's heart, the *Mayflower* and the *Speedwell* set sail to the west. (They were using a different calendar system than the Gregorian calendar in use today. All dates in this book are the dates of the old calendar. To convert them, add ten days. August 5 would be August 15 in the modern calendar.) The winds were with them, warm and westbound. The *Mayflower* took to the high seas well. But during the first three hundred miles it gradually became undeniable that the *Speedwell* had been poorly named. The only thing the *Speedwell* did well was leak. She clearly would not make it across the ocean without extensive repair. Both ships jibbed around and sailed back to England, the *Speedwell's* crew bailing as she went. They put in at Dartmouth, the port at the mouth of the River Dart on the southern coast of England. Carpenters examined every inch of the hull. They couldn't find many actual leaks, but in one place they found a hole two feet long, patched with a board so rotten they could peel it off with their fingers.

Deathly sick and full of dread, Robert Cushman wrote to a friend:

> . . .*For besides the eminent dangers of this voyage, which are no less than deadly, an infirmity of body hath seized me, which will not in all likelihood leave me till death. What to call it I know not, but it is a bundle of lead, as it were, crushing my heart more and more these fourteen days; as that although I do the actions of a living man, yet I am but as dead, but the will of God be done. Our pinnace will not cease leaking, else I think we had been halfway at Virginia. Our voyage hither hath been as full of crosses as ourselves have been of crookedness.*

In writing "full of crosses" Cushman referred to the cross of Christ, the one on which they all seemed to be so consistently crucified. Someone fearing witchcraft might use the word "jinxed." He and other passengers were interpreting the problems upon problems as foreboding hints of a trajectory aimed at nothing less than disaster. By "crookedness," he meant the questionable finances of Christopher Martin. "He so insulteth over our poor people with such scorn and contempt," Cushman wrote, "as if they were not enough to wipe his shoes."

As they lay up in Dartmouth, four days of westbound wind blew by. Cushman, in his pain, dismay and self-pity, did not doubt that the next four days would be wasted as well. Meanwhile, as they waited on repairs, the passengers dug into the food supply. "Our victuals will be half eaten up, I think, before we go from the coast of England," Cushman wrote, "and if our voyage last long, we shall not have a month's victuals when we come in the country."

Despite the warmth of August, winter was, in a sense, coming on. The voyage was going to take at least two months, maybe three, and then they'd have to find a place to settle, and by the time they got their goods ashore, trees felled, houses built, firewood cut, they might well be working in the flurries of late autumn. Planting was already out of the question. Between the delays and the leaky ship, passengers were having second thoughts. Some were ready to write off their investments or pay for what they'd already eaten, but Martin wouldn't listen to them, wouldn't even let them get off the ship lest they never come back. Even the sailors were getting angry at him as he tried to boss them around and tell them how to sail.

Worsening the stress, many passengers suspected that the sailors of the *Speedwell*, maybe even the captain, were *making* the ship leak. Why else would it leak so bad at sea but not in port? As it became increasingly obvious that the ships might have to winter over in Virginia and that food supplies were already running low, the crew was reluctant to start the voyage. Even William Bradford suspected the crew of sabotaging their own ship.

They got the *Speedwell* patched up and bailed out, and off they went again. And again, she proved as seaworthy as a sieve. Barely a hundred leagues (three hundred miles) into the thousand-league voyage, the ships turned around again, bailed back to England, this time putting in at Plymouth.

Cushman was now sure that not only was he on his deathbed but that his deathbed was on a sinking ship. Again workmen searched for leaks but found none, just a hull full of water. The captain and crew agreed that the *Speedwell* was too small for the wider sails that had been retrofitted for the oceanic voyage. The pressure of the wind against the sail opened stressed the timbers of the hull, opening leaks all over the place. In other words, they had themselves a lemon. She was strictly for local hauls. The *Mayflower*, it was decided, would have to go alone; the *Speedwell* would head back to London for easier chores. (Despite its sorry shape, the *Speedwell*, given sails more suited to her size, would perform well in local waters for years to come. Crewmembers would later admit that they had exaggerated the leaking to free themselves from the probable need to suffer a year in America.)

The question, then, was how many people could be packed into the *Mayflower* and who those people would be. They knew of the perils of an overloaded ship. In 1618, the Protestant Reverend Francis Blackwell had set out from Amsterdam for Virginia with 180 people. By the time they spied land, the Reverend Blackwell, the ship's captain, and 130 other people had died of illness and dehydration.

Over the next few days the Planters transferred some of the cargo from the *Speedwell* to the *Mayflower* and decided who would go to America now, who would go later, who never. The decisions must have come out of a chaotic and emotional negotiation of goods, refunds, promises, and desperate decisions. Bradford wrote that a good many people were relieved not to have to make the trip. "Those who went back [to London] were for the most part such as were willing so to do, either out of some discontent or fear they conceived of the ill success of the voyage, seeing so may crosses befall, and the year time so far spent."

In some cases, whole families opted to stay in England. Others insisted on sticking together for the trip. Others divided, with one or both parents going, maybe one or the other staying, their children directed to remain or get back on the ship. Christopher Martin and family were among those who stayed together for the trip. Master Reynolds, who had sailed the *Speedwell* from Holland, decided to stay in England. Robert Cushman stayed behind, though he failed to die as soon as he had feared. He would arrive on the next ship to New England, a few weeks late for Thanksgiving.

So the *Mayflower* was rather crowded, and the provisions for their first year in Virginia were now definitely less than sufficient. We do not know exactly what the hold held, but in 1629, the *Talbut*, a ship of the *Mayflower*'s size that happened to carry a hundred passengers on a one-way trip to America, with only the crew returning to England, carried the following:

> 11,340 gallons of beer in 45 tuns
> 1,512 gallons of water in 6 tuns
> 22 hogshead of beef
> 12,000 pounds of bread

40 bushes of peas

20 bushels of oatmeal

4,500 lbs. of haberdyne fish

8 dozen pounds of candles

2 barrels of beer vinegar

1-1/2 bushels mustard seed

20 gallons of olive oil

2 barrels of soap

90 gallons of butter in 10 barrels

100 lbs. cheese

20 gallons aquavit

Firewood fr six weeks of cooking

The *Talbut* also carried several barrels of wine. No documents from Plymouth indicate wine on the *Mayflower*, but beer was a daily staple for everyone, including children. The *Mayflower* may have carried enough to provide everyone with a gallon a day for several months.

The *Mayflower* also took tools and supplies that the Planters would use to build houses, clear forest, and plant gardens and fields. They had several muskets and a good supply of gunpowder. They had at least one large screw-type jack for lifting the beams of houses. Inexplicably, they brought no small fishhooks — possibly an oversight, possibly just one of those things that got left on the *Speedwell*.

The ship probably carried a few farm animals, too, but the only record is of two dogs: a mastiff bitch and a spaniel. The livestock most likely included chickens, pigs, and goats — generally smaller animals that would better survive a long trip in a small ship and that would need little open pasturage in a land covered with forest.

The ship almost certainly had a cat as part of its crew. A ship without a cat soon became a ship with fat rats and no food. Without cats, transoceanic navigation would have been impossible. The settlers probably had a cat or two as well. In that cats have accompanied every advance of civilization, and rats have either been there waiting or followed along, the settlers would have been foolish to attempt a new colony without something to keep the rodents under control. We have no records attesting to the presence or absence of cats, but the survival of the colony and the absence of any reference to rats implies that if a cat did not arrive with the *Mayflower*, one arrived soon after.

The *Mayflower* carried no bees. The settlers probably didn't know that North America had no honeybees and thus little or no honey, a great source of imperishable food energy. Bees also pollinate the garden crops that the Planters planned to plant. (Other kinds of bees produce honey, but not enough to harvest.) Corn, which is pollinated not by bees but by the wind, was already growing quite well in

New England. Fruits, vegetables, and berries were being pollinated by various insects, from butterflies to non-honey bees, but these crops do much better with a little assistance from the fuzzy, pollen-catching legs of Europe's *Apis mellifera*. Eventually a ship would bring a few hives full of bees. The hives would be sealed shut for the whole voyage, the bees living off their combs of honey. Once in America, each swarm could be divided once or twice a year. Inevitably swarms would flee their hives, and soon wild honeybees would populate the continent.

The passengers built small "cabins" in their sliver of space between the main deck and the hold. These cabins were no bigger than a bunk or two. The stacking of passengers in bunk beds would have opened up a little more space on the deck. Families and unmarried girls had the privilege and privacy of cabins. Dozens of other people hunkered down wherever they found enough deck space to sit. Banned from the upper deck during bad weather or turbulent seas, they may have remained in the crowded and perpetual dusk for days on end. For their unmentionable discharges, they used chamber pots. For washing body and clothes, they waited.

They ate what the ship's cook brought them — perhaps a paste-thick pea soup flavored with peppercorn (black pepper) and bits of salted cod, beef or pork, perhaps a rock-hard unleavened biscuit soaked in beer, perhaps oatmeal or a porridge of ground barley or wheat, perhaps a gruel of rice and marrow. Olive oil and vinegar added a little extra flavor. They ate off trenchers, wooden plates a little deep in the center, some with a little crater on the side to hold a bit of salt. If they wanted spice — a bit of salt, a pinch of sugar, a herb — they had to use their own. They didn't drink much, if any, water, nor had they ever. The waters of London and any town were as foul and toxic as sewage. Even fresh spring water would go bad in a barrel after a few weeks. So they drank beer, a beverage of palpable vivacity whose microbes had died in the boiling of the malt and whose alcoholic content prevented spoilage. Beer was part of a healthy breakfast, an early dose of carbohydrates, not to mention good cheer. It would not be unusual for a man to drink a gallon a day. From infancy on, the passengers of the *Mayflower* knew the comfort of mild inebriation.

Chapter Five

The People

History has come to know this whole group as the Pilgrims. The closest they came to seeing themselves as such was reflected in a line in Bradford's *Of Plymouth Plantation*: "So they left that goodly and pleasant city [Leyden] which had been their resting place near twelve years; but they knew they were pilgrims, and looked not much on those things, but lift up their eyes to the heavens, their dearest country, and quieted their spirits." This was apparently a reference to two lines in the Geneva Bible, Hebrews xi, 13-14: *All these died in faith, and received not the promises, but saw them afar off, and believed them, and received them thankfully, and confessed that they were strangers and pilgrims on the earth. For they that say such things, declare plainly, that they seek a country.*

So if these people saw themselves as pilgrims, it wasn't as pilgrims on a pilgrimage from Europe to America. They were unsettled people on Earth, unattached to places or things, passing through on their way to Heaven. Or at least thirty-seven of them were. As many as sixty-four others were just looking for something that London didn't offer. Bradford would refer to these people as "strangers." Twenty-five or thirty others — the number is unknown — were sailors who just wanted to make their wages and go home.

Forty-one of the hundred and two passengers were men twenty-one years of age or older. The average age of those whose ages we know was about thirty-four. Eighteen passengers were adult women, all married. We don't know the ages of everyone, but apparently of the thirty boys under twenty-one, almost half were not yet adolescents. Of the thirteen unmarried girls, four were adolescents. Several men left wives behind, and some of couples left children, too. Three men came with teenage sons. Five young children came without their parents.

Richard Warren left his wife, Elizabeth, and five daughters. Francis Cooke left his wife, Hester, and four children, but he took his son John, who was thirteen or fourteen years old. Degory Priest left his wife, Sarah, and two daughters.

Thomas Rogers took his son, left a wife and two daughters. William and Dorothy Bradford left their three-year-old son John behind. The Brewsters took Love and Wrestling but left Fear, Jonathan and Patience behind.

Samuel and Katherine More didn't go, didn't even want to go. They had no religious issues to resolve, no need of a better life. They already had a pretty good life, at least in terms of stuff. Their problem was divorce, a particularly scandalous one. Some of their four children — maybe all of them — turned out to be hers but quite possibly not his. The biological daddy may have lived right next door. To relieve themselves of this problem and spare the children the embarrassment of bastardy, they gave all four to Separatists and paid the children's one-way passage to a place from which they weren't likely to return. Ellen, 8, went with the family of Edward Winslow. Jasper, 7, went with the Carvers. Richard, 6, and Mary, 4, were handed over to the Brewsters.

Little Humility Cooper also went without her parents. Her father had died, and her mother, for reasons today unknown, gave her to her uncle and aunt, Edward and Ann (Cooper) Tilley. Barely weaned from her mother's breast, she set off for North America. Though probably the youngest to board the *Mayflower* - little Samuel Eaton may have been a bit younger - neither he nor she would be the youngest to disembark in America.

Elizabeth Hopkins, Mary Allerton and Susanna White boarded the *Mayflower* pregnant.

Desire Minter, a teenager, went for much the same reason as Humility Cooper. She had buried her father in Leyden, and her mother had decided to remain there with him. She sent the girl off to support herself in a place where God would be more accessible. Under the wing or employ of John Carver's family, Desire would have constituted half an adult, entitling Carver to half a share in the venture's profit. In seven years she would be a free woman, albeit with little to show for her efforts.

Only two other girls were of marriageable age. One, Dorothy, was a servant to the Carver family. The other, Priscilla, daughter of William and Alice Mullins, was about sixteen. Desire, Dorothy and Priscilla boarded the ship with over fifty men who had no wives, at least none with them.

Not one passenger claimed the rights of noble birth or the authority of government title. None could claim a station above middle class. All but a handful were blue-collar tradesmen. They were, for the most part, venture capitalists without capital and nothing to venture but their labor and lives.

William Brewster was one of the oldest of the passengers, probably about fifty-four. (John Carver was about fity-five; James Chilton was around sixty-four; one or two others may have been about that old.) As a founder of the Separatist congregation in Scrooby and Elder of the church in Leyden, Brewster oversaw the behavior of his flock. He offered advice on issues of morality and admonishment for moral shortcomings. He was not, however, a pastor.

William Bradford had no title in the church, but he'd been among its most active members. He was twenty-three when he married a sixteen-year-old, Dorothy. They soon had a baby and named him John. Little John was three years old when his parents kissed him good-bye.

Myles Standish, in charge of security, held the kind of physical power that any military leader holds. He had his own weapons, including flintlock muskets and a sword long enough to skewer a bear. He knew how to use his weapons. Little is known of his life before he boarded the *Mayflower*. He was probably about thirty-six years old and had known combat in his defense of England in battles with the Spanish in Holland. He may have come from Lancashire or the Isle of Man. He was short and bearded, his face the color of a parboiled shrimp. He could quickly lose his temper over issues of stupidity or insolence. Years later, William Hubbard would write, in *A General History of New England*, "A little chimney is soon fired; so was the Plymouth captain, a

72

man of very little stature, yet of a very hot and angry temper. The fire of his passion soon kindled, and blown up into a flame by hot words, might easily have consumed all, had it not been seasonably quenched." Once they got to know him, the settlers might well have worried about such a man being the most powerful among them.

Stephen Hopkins, who had worked as a merchant and clerk, was the only passenger with experience on the American continent. He'd sailed to Jamestown in 1609. Along the way, his ship wrecked on the Isle of Devils, in the Bermudas. There he, the crew, and several passengers spent ten months living off turtles, birds, mollusks, and wild pigs. When Hopkins got caught trying to organize a mutiny against the governor — actually he just wanted to separate from the others and stay in Bermuda — the governor sentenced him to death. He wept and pleaded his way out of it, however, and the stranded survivors finally managed to build two boats that took them to Virginia. Hopkins eventually returned to England to find that his wife had died. In due time, he married a widow, Elizabeth Fisher, who soon bore a child, her first. He, Elizabeth, and their three children, Constance, fourteen, Giles, twelve, and Damaris, one, all signed up for the *Mayflower* and the adventure in America. Elizabeth was seven or eight months pregnant when she waddled up the gangplank for the last time, no doubt wondering whether this trip was a good idea.

John Carver and Christopher Martin had risen a bit above the working class. Carver and his wife, Katherine, had no children but took as servants John Howland, about twenty-one, William Latham, eleven, Roger Wilder, also a minor, and the young Desire Minter. It is unclear to what extent the Carvers considered these young people family, servants, or apprentices.

A few others took servants. Stephen Hopkins took Edward Doty and Edward Leister. William and Susanna White took William Holbeck. Christopher Martin took John Langmore. Samuel Fuller, deacon, took William Butten. William Mullins, a shoemaker and shoe salesman, took Robert Carter, two hundred and fifty shoes and thirteen pairs of boots.

Just about everyone else was a tradesman, farmer, merchant, or general roustabout. William Brewster had studied at Cambridge and worked for England's secretary of state. He later became a printer and publisher, specializing in religious issues, which is what had gotten him into trouble in Holland and left him a wanted man in England. William Bradford was a fustian weaver, Francis Cooke a wool comber, James Chilton a tailor. Edward Winslow helped Brewster in the printing business. John Turner was a merchant. Francis Eaton was a house carpenter. John Alden, a barrel-maker, was hired to serve as ship's cooper. Isaac Allerton was a tailor. John Allerton, who may have been Isaac's brother, was a seaman. William Trevore was hired by the group to work as a laborer and seaman. Thomas Tinker sawed wood. Nothing is known of Thomas Rogers's profession, but according to tax records, the wife and children he left in Leyden were considered "poor." No one represented the government, a company, or any church save that of the essentially unstructured Separatist congregation. No one was paid to be a leader. They did not consider themselves equals, but they recognized that they were all in the same boat, none of them riding first class, all of them sharing a single debt, all of them bound for the same place and bound to suffer the same hardships. No one, apparently, intended to get rich quick on gold or the labor of slaves and then return to England.

So the *Mayflower* contained a cross-section of values that would become quintessentially American: the insistence on following the heart rather than the law; the inability to tolerate injustice; the audacity to demand authority over authorities; the courage to pursue happiness no matter how miserable it might make them, and to seek a better life no matter how much worse it might be; the wisdom of working together as a society for mutual benefit and personal profit. They believed in the power of the congregation. They would do their own thinking and make their own decisions. They would pray their own prayers. They would dig in their heels. The strong would bury the weak, perhaps suffer a moment of doubt, then remember the mercy of their God, and then get back to work.

Chapter Six

The Crossing

Someone in this group kept a journal of that first year. It would return to England aboard the *Fortune* in December 1621. Within a year it would be published in London in 1622 under the title *Mourt's Relation.* We do not know who "Mourt" was. No one of that name went to America on the *Mayflower.* A "G. Mourt" signed a "To the Reader" introduction to the book. It is widely supposed that the name is a pseudonym for a publisher named George Morton. The publisher may have used a pseudonym due to the dubious legality of the Separatist settlement and the possible guilt by association of anyone who promoted their venture.

In all likelihood, the book has several authors. It includes a few letters signed with initials — two letters apparently by Robert Cushman, one by pastor John Robinson (who had remained in Leyden), and one by Edward Winslow. The main narrative of the book, however, has no names or initials to indicate an author. This narrative, a journal divided into five parts, reports events from the September 6, 1620 launch of the *Mayflower* until an expedition to the Massachusetts tribe in September, 1621. The most likely journalists are Edward Winslow and William Bradford. Governor John Carver may have contributed. The journalist or journalists tended to write in the first person plural — *we* — and the third person plural — *they*. Nowhere does a sentence use the pronoun *I*. In a few cases, *he* apparently refers to the writer himself and *they* includes the author. In many cases, a confusion of pronouns leaves us wondering who did what and exactly what happened.

The journalists may have written the narrative for various reasons. In the tradition of explorers, they may have been reporting on events and discoveries. They may have been reporting to investors. They may have been encouraging more people to come join the colony. As a real estate advertisement, however, it fails. It reports much suffering, alludes to much danger, and hints at the difficulties of starting from scratch under the duress of New England weather. Alas, it also falls short of an ideal history. It provides a bounty of information, but it leaves out such obviously significant details as the dates of deaths. It mentions only a few of the people who died and nothing about grief or burials. It reports little about the activities of daily life and the human conflicts that inevitably arise among people under great stress. Except for a quick allusion to a conflict just before they landed at Cape Cod, it mentions no arguments or disagreements. It expresses no regrets, misgivings, or second thoughts. It rarely mentions women and children. It says nothing of hunger. It admits to considerable suffering, but we have to look between the lines to imagine the conditions that killed so many people in so little time. If *Mourt's Relation* sold any real estate, it was only by neglecting to mention the absolute worst of the experience.

Mourt's Relation relates little about the voyage across the Atlantic. In sixty-seven words, it takes us from the launch on September 6 to the first sighting of land on November 9. That same sentence brushes off two months of terror and hardship with just five words: ...*many difficulties in boisterous storms*... One of those many difficulties would be the sheer stress of knowing that they had shoved off two months later than planned. They would arrive on the verge of winter with dwindling food supplies, no homes on shore, no friends outside their group, and no possibility of going back until, at best, spring. But the option of sailing toward difficulties seemed better than the pressures pushing them from behind: persecution by the king, financial demands from their backers, the sale of most of their possessions to pay for the trip, the lack of jobs or houses to go back to, the frustrations of delay, and the certainty that a cold and hungry winter in a strange land was safer than worship with a papal flavor.

While *Mourt's Relation* tells us little of the voyage, another source, William Bradford's *Of Plymouth Plantation 1620 – 1647*, gives us more details. He tells us that for the first few days, they sailed before a "prosperous wind" that did much encourage them. But prosperous winds didn't keep them from throwing up all over the place. Restricted to the windowless gun deck, unable to orient their balance to the horizon, the passengers suffered explosive bouts of seasickness. Without benefit of portholes or anything that would flush, they heaved their beer-soaked biscuits, their bits of cod, their oatmeal, pea porridge, and salted pork. Maybe Brewster offered a psalm to assuage them: *He shows by the sea what care God has over man, for when he delivers them from the great danger of the sea, he delivers them as it were from a thousand deaths. They mount up to the heaven, they go down again to the depths: their soul is melted because of trouble.*

An especially obnoxious sailor did what he could to

make them feel worse.

> *...he would always be condemning the poor people in their sickness and cursing them daily with grievous execrations; and did not let to tell that he hoped to help cast half of them overboard before they came to their journey's end, and to make merry with what they had, and if he were by any gently reproved, he would curse and swear most bitterly. But it pleased God before they came half seas over, to smite this young man with a grievous disease, of which he died in a desperate manner, and so was himself the first that was thrown overboard. Thus his curses light on his own head, and it was astonishment to all his fellows for they noted it to be the just hand of God upon him.*

For the next two months the passengers would live in a dim, wet world that smelled of seawater, vomit, chamber pots, animal dung, unwashed clothes, and every aroma the human body can produce, not to mention whiffs of the wine, tar, fish, and turpentine of cargoes past. They heard men snore, women weep, children whine, an oink-oink here, a cluck-cluck there, sailors thumping around the deck above. They heard each other pray. They heard the stutter of the tiller as it swung back and forth at the rear of the gundeck. They heard a continuous creaking of wood that spoke of the condition of the ship, the mood of the sea, the strength of the wind. Sometimes the creaking murmured that all was well; sometimes it screamed that man was not meant to sail across oceans. They read the tones of the shouts of the sailors to guess the ever-shifting degree of danger. When waves reared back and thundered across the upper deck, cold water dripped through the decking. During each four-hour shift, sailors manned two pumps to draw the water out of the bilge, up onto the top deck, where most of it ran to the sea but some of it dripped or trickled back down on the passengers. The passengers were moist at the best of times, soaked at the worst of times, and never truly dry, not for a moment, from late summer 1620 until mid-winter 1621.

During calm weather Master Jones may have let passengers come up onto the main deck for a bit of air, light, and exercise. At any sign of bad weather or any need to work with rigging, passengers had to descend immediately to their dim, dank quarters. If bad weather threatened, the crew fit the lids over the hatch, letting the passengers ride out the storm in the dusky gun deck.

The ship never stopped, never dropped anchor, never rested motionless. The passengers spent the entire voyage swinging between extremes of boredom and fear. Except for the occasional moment on deck, calm seas meant endless hours of sitting in one place, talking to the same people about a daily routine that never changed. But none would wish for more interesting weather. Winds brought waves that took the ship on a terrifying ride. The prosperous winds turned ferocious as the ship sailed into the middle of hurricane season. By sheer luck — or was it miracle? — the *Mayflower* would spend over two months in the North Atlantic without getting hit by weather of hurricane strength, but something mighty strong hit them, and more than once. Somewhere midatlantic, the *Mayflower*, so tall and solid at the dock, all but cowered under mountainous waves. At times the wind pushed her over so far that the mainyard, the fifty-foot horizontal yardarm from which the mainsail hung some forty feet above the deck, would lean over and grab the water. As the water pulled at it, it acted as a twenty-five-foot lever that tugged violently at the mast, making the whole ship shudder and groan as if trying not to tear in half. More than once Master Jones gave up trying to control the ship. When the wind grew too fierce, he gave the order to go "at hull." Working in a murderous wind, the crew pulled down all sails and every possible piece of rigging, reducing the ship to not much more than a hull with a barely waterproof lid. They lashed everything down tight, battened the hatches, barred the doors, tucked themselves into the forecastle, put out the fire, and prayed for God to do what Man couldn't. They feared a wave swamping the ship and dashing it to pieces. They feared broken masts and yards. They feared the wave that would lift the ship at one end but not the other, leaving one half of her supported by water, the other half sticking out into the air. She was a ship, not a bridge, built to be cradled, not suspended. The unsupported weight could well crack her in half. To avoid such structural stress, the helmsman would turn the ship to take the waves broadside.

But the broadside pounding put a lot of pressure against the beams that arched under the main deck and kept the hull from breaking inward. One beam, oak half a foot or more thick, warped and bowed as it took punch after punch from thousands of tons of water. The passengers didn't know much about ships, but they knew beams weren't supposed to warp. They also knew scared sailors when they saw them. With typical understatement, Bradford wrote, "there was great distraction and difference of opinion amongst the mariners themselves." The leaders of the passengers entered into consultation with Master Jones and his mates, suggested that maybe it might be wise to turn around and go back, that maybe King James was less dangerous than an angry sea. But Jones told them that they were already closer to the New World than the Old. He thought his *May-*

flower was actually in pretty good condition and taking the seas well. He'd seen her take a pounding like this for two weeks off the coast of Norway, but he'd eventually brought her into port. They might as well go west as east.

The *Mayflower* was probably at hull when a wave slugged her especially hard at just the right angle. The bent oak beam cracked like a cannon shot. As wave after wave washed over the topdeck, fear and cold water flooded down to the gun deck, inundating the terrified passengers, soaking everything as it sloshed back and forth across the deck. The ship's carpenter no doubt raced to the scene and was surely relieved to see water coming down instead of up. Still, it was a grave situation. With one beam broken, the others held less lateral pressure against the hull. Another good whack from the outside could snap another beam. In a matter of minutes, the *Mayflower* could crack in half, break up in the tumult of wind and waves, leaving a hundred-odd people foundering a thousand miles from land, clinging to each other and to pieces of wreckage, gradually weakening and watching each other disappear. But someone remembered the large house jack that had come on board. This was its moment in history. With wet and desperate shoulders and some fast turning of the jack, they forced the beam back into position, propped it with a post, and nailed it with a multitude of prayers, perhaps a psalm: *They that go down to the sea in ships, that do business in great waters; He shows by the sea what care God has over man, for when he delivers them from the great danger of the sea, he delivers them as it were from a thousand deaths.*

The beam held.

The *Mayflower* almost lost a passenger when John Howland went up on deck during heavy weather. As the ship rolled to one side, Howland slipped into the sea. Though he was powerless to resist the waves, the topsail halyard, which happened to be trailing in the water, happened to come into his hand, which he happened to close at the right moment. He held it as he sank what seemed to him several fathoms. The crew hauled him to the surface and used a boat hook or something to bring him up to the deck. Bradford described him as "something ill with it," as anyone might be after being snatched back from sure death. But he got over it. It may be a good thing he did. Within his cold, wet breeches he carried the genetic roots of the forty-first and forty-third presidents of the United States, George H.W. Bush and his son. Howland was also an ancestor of Edith Roosevelt, wife of Theodore.

Somewhere between England and America, Elizabeth Hopkins, wife of Stephen, mother of Damaris and stepmother of Constance and Giles, went into labor and delivered a baby boy. We do not know the date or the weather. The ship may have been smoothly tacking to the west, or it may have been in the throes of a storm. They named the boy Oceanus. His mother's breast may have tasted slightly of seawater.

The passenger population of the *Mayflower* returned to 102 with the death of William Butten, who expired on November 6. He was young, a servant to deacon Fuller. Nothing else is known of him. In all likelihood he was buried at sea. Passengers were probably allowed on deck to witness his shrouded body being lowered into the cold waves. Or maybe they watched from the gun deck as he was slid out a gun port. Separatists would not perform a religious ceremony — none was prescribed in their Bible — but passengers of the Church of England might have liked a traditional good-bye. As Master of the ship, Christopher Jones may have read from the Book of Common Prayer. William Brewster, in his capacity as Elder, may have later talked of life and death in a sermon, perhaps offering a piece of a psalm: *For he is content with that life that God gives for by death the shortness of this life is recompensed with immortality.*

Master Jones had to make this voyage with the simplest of navigation equipment. For direction, of course, he used a simple compass — a sliver of iron magnetized by the stroking of a lodestone. But the compass did not always point at the lodestar, the north star, Polaris. Magnetic north is neither below that star nor directly on the northernmost point of the planet. Rather, magnetic north wanders around the northern longitudes. Navigators had no idea why Plymouth (the one in New England, not old England) was at 18 degrees, 40 minutes in 1605 but at 13 degrees 40 minutes in 1620. A compass might bring a ship close to Plymouth, but the unpredictable variation in magnetic north could mean the difference between sailing in the ocean and sailing on a beach.

Knowing one's direction is of little use if one does not know how far one has gone in that direction. True, if a ship left Europe and sailed straight west (which, due to wind directions and water currents, it couldn't really do), it would eventually hit the landmass of the Americas. Hitting a landmass, however, is something seamen have traditionally tried to avoid. For obvious reasons, coming close is preferable. It is also preferable to arrive near the destination rather than taking a long and dangerous trip up or down the coast.

Measuring distance to the east or west was not easy. Neither the *Mayflower* nor any other ship of the time was able to calculate longitude at sea. To do so would require a genius as yet unborn and a clock as yet uninvented. Astronomers could measure the longitude of any place that had an accurate clock, but the constant tilting of a ship

at sea made a mockery of pendulums. The only way to es-
timate longitude was to physically measure the distance
sailed from a starting point at a known longitude, a process
called dead reckoning. This measurement was made more
complicated by a ship's inability to sail straight into the
wind. It could sail west in an eastbound wind, but to do so
it had to tack slightly northwest and southwest, back and
forth, using the rudder and the angle of the sails to cut a
course against the wind. The navigator would have to measure the distance sailed to the northwest and then to the
southwest, then figure in the angle, then calculate how far
due west the ship had actually gone.

The ship measured distance by dropping a triangular
chip of weighted wood into the ocean and letting a nine-
hundred-foot log-line feed out from a reel as the ship sailed
away from it. The line had knots at certain intervals. They
could be counted as they slipped through a man's fingers.
But this measurement alone was hardly accurate. The ship
was not on a stable platform. It was in water, and the water
was moving. Navigators already knew more or less the direction that the ocean flowed at various points. In the North
Atlantic, the Gulf Stream moved northeast off the coast of
Virginia, then turned more to the east, then more to the
north as if aiming to slip between the British Isles and Ice-
land. Water on the northern edge of that current peeled off

to the north and west to flow up around the west coast of Greenland. There it passed a current coming down the east coast of northern Canada to curl around Newfoundland and down the coast of New England, just inside the northbound Gulf Stream. Closer to Europe, waters on the southeastern side of the Gulf Stream veered off to the south to sweep past Spain, Saharan Africa, and the Canary islands. There the current turned west toward the Caribbean. By knowing which current the ship was in, a navigator could assume that the ship was drifting in a certain direction at a certain immeasurable speed.

The navigator could measure speed two ways. One was by periodic calculation of changes in latitude, though that didn't really measure the ship's speed forward, not unless it was going due north or south. The other way was to count the knots in the log-line over a period of time. They used an hourglass to measure that time. By dividing the distance by the time, they calculated speed in "knots" per hour. If they knew the speed and it seemed to be constant, they wouldn't need to measure each and every nautical mile.

Determining latitude — one's distance from the equator — was a lot easier than calculating longitude. It wasn't necessary to measure physical distance traveled. Master Jones needed nothing more than a cross staff — a yard-long vertical staff with a horizontal crosspiece that slid up and down the staff. The vertical staff was marked in degrees. At noon — that is, the moment when the sun was highest in the sky, not necessarily at the moment the clock would have struck twelve if they'd had a clock — he would aim the crosspiece at the horizon, the vertical piece at the sun. The angle, noted in numerical charts and duly calculated, indicated the degrees north of the equator.

They measured depth with a 150-fathom line weighted with lead. This instrument was known informally as a dipsie. Nine hundred feet of water wouldn't be of immediate concern to a ship that needed just twelve feet to float, but any indication of ground beneath the sea was reason for people to start paying attention.

So Master Jones had to navigate across the North Atlantic using nothing but a few pieces of wood, a long string, a sliver of iron and a jar of sand. The ship would have to sail a constant zigzag as it tacked against the prevailing westerly wind, the general northeasterly flow of weather and water that followed the Gulf Stream, and the vast counterclockwise cyclones that swirled up from the south. Storms blew the ship off course and made it difficult or impossible to keep track of distance. Clouds hid the heavens and horizon for days at a time, rendering the cross staff useless. The Gulf Stream constantly nudged the ship to the north and east.

Jones knew where he was going, but history does not know the course he took. He may have followed Columbus's route, riding the Canaries Current to the Canary Islands off the coast of Morocco at latitude 29 degrees, about as far north as Tampa, Florida. From there he would have sailed west around the bottom of the dead-calm, weed-choked Sargasso Sea, then turned northeast to take advantage of the Gulf Stream. Or as most ships bound for New England and Virginia did, he may have sailed southwest to the Azores, a thousand miles off the coast of Portugal at 38 degrees, then almost due west. Or he may have taken the shortest route, the great-circle around the north, where the globe narrows, to come down south on the Arctic current past Newfoundland — a tricky, risky route not recommended for a ship that could not calculate longitude. Whatever his course, Master Jones took sixty-five days to bring his ship and all his passengers, save young Butten, plus young Oceanus, minus the sailor who had died, to the coast of North America just one half of one degree north of his destination. He had aimed at the mouth of the Hudson but arrived a hundred miles north at Cape Cod. Had he sailed in an impossibly straight line from Plymouth to Plymouth, he'd have sailed about 2,750 miles. If we assume that tacking added 250 miles and that storms didn't blow him too far off course, we bring the total to a hypothetical but conveniently round total of about 3,000. The *Mayflower's* average speed, then, would be a little under two miles an hour.

While they were on deck on November 6 to bid God-be to William Butten, the passengers may have noticed something changing. Master Jones most certainly noticed a change in cloud formation as the Westerlies off the continent hit the warm air over the Gulf Stream. As soundings found the bottom of the ocean, he'd have his crew alert for rocks and shoals. The crew would have noticed a change in the color of the water, and maybe even the passengers would smell the sweet air coming off the land. And on November 9, someone high in the rigging probably really did shout, "Land Ho!" Permitted or not, passengers could not have resisted coming up through the hatch to have a look at the New World. Quite likely they all rushed up and pressed to the railing, looking west. Their weight may well have tilted the ship to that side. At first it would have been hard to see, but as they crept closer at two excruciating slow miles per hour, they would soon glimpse the low, sandy hills of Cape Cod.

Chapter Seven

Association and Agreement

I n words worthy of a poet, William Bradford wrote a para-
graph about their arrival:

> *Being thus passed the vast ocean, and a sea*
> *of troubles before in their preparation (as may*
> *be remembered by that which went before), they*
> *had now no friends to welcome them nor inns to*
> *entertain or refresh their weather-beaten bod-*
> *ies; no houses or much less towns to repair to,*
> *to see for succour....for which way soever they*
> *turned their eyes (save upward to the heavens)*
> *they could have little solace or content in respect*
> *of any outward objects. For summer being done,*

all things stand upon them with a weatherbeaten face, and the whole country, full of woods and thickets, represented a wild and savage hue. If they looked behind them, there was the mighty ocean which they had passed and was not as a main bar and gulf to separate them from all the civil parts of the world.

But they weren't home yet. Cape Cod wasn't where they were going. They were going to Virginia. Technically they were in Virginia — that is, territory claimed by the king of England — but they'd had their eye on the Virginia south of the Hudson, the area covered by the Virginia Company's patent, the area where they had permission to settle.

Jones turned the *Mayflower* south. Within a day the ship fell among dangerous shoals and roaring breakers. The *Mayflower* was, as their journalist noted, so far entangled therewith that the passengers conceived themselves in great danger. The French and Dutch knew these shoals as Malabar. The Pilgrims called them Tucker's Terrour. With the wind diminishing and the sun sinking just as he needed both to navigate out of danger, Jones turned north and east. As the moon that night would not rise until after midnight, he probably dropped anchor not long after the 4:35 sunset. Judging by the time it took him to reach Cape Cod from Tucker's Terror, we can surmise that he enjoyed a southerly wind on November 10 and spent a long night at anchor. Early on November 11, the ship curled around the tip of Cape Cod to drop anchor in the calm haven of its embrace.

And there they were.

The group had a patent to settle in Virginia under the purview of the Virginia Company. Their effort to reach northern area of Virginia, however, seems to have been somewhat less than half-hearted. They had crossed the ocean, but now some shoals had discouraged them from going the extra hundred miles south. Jones would have gone, but his passengers liked the look of Cape Cod Bay. They would sail no more.

Had they intended to settle there all along? They may have known about the place from John Smith's *Description of New England*. He had called it "the Paradise of all those parts." It was cooler than Jamestown and warmer than Maine. He marveled at the corn planted around the harbor off the coast of the place inhabited by the Massachusetts. He complimented the kindness of the people. He mapped a certain place that Prince Charles named Plimouth. Smith described Plimouth as "an excellent good harbor, good land, and no want of anything except industrious people." The *Mayflower* almost certainly carried a copy of Smith's book and his map.

So when a boatload of industrious people came looking for a place to hang their collective shingle, New England's Plimouth may have called a little more sweetly than the territory of the Virginia Company. (The place would be known by various names: Plymouth, New Plymouth, Plimoth, New Plimoth, Plimmouth, and New Plimmouth. Apparently Americans have had trouble spelling since Day One.)

Any such intention to avoid Virginia and sail directly to Plimouth, however, is pure conjecture. No evidence indicates that they aimed for that area. But once they were there, they wondered why they couldn't settle outside the bounds of the Virginia Company. After all, the Company hadn't really done anything to deserve their loyalty. At most it offered, through its patent, a corporate governance that carried much obligation on the settlers' part while offering little protection or backing by the Company. As the settlers in Jamestown had learned, the protection and backing weren't necessarily there when needed.

The passengers were unsure of the governance situation in New England. It was the king's territory, of course, but they didn't know the status of the current patent. Sir Ferdinando Gorges had applied for authority over the area under the Council for New England, but when the *Mayflower* set sail, the king had not yet given the council a grant for the territory. The grant was, in fact, given before the *Mayflower* arrived at Cape Cod, but the settlers had no way of knowing that. They were out to sea, a world away, on their own, trying to figure out the right thing to do. As far as they knew, there was no authority from which they should request a patent to settle there. They had no authority supporting or protecting them. Thus it could be argued that they owed no obligation to anyone. They'd found this land. They were there. No one else was. Arguably, it was theirs.

Not that they gave the thought much consideration, but still, the implications were staggering. Though it was the king's territory, no one had currently staked it out for settlement (no one in Europe, anyway). It wasn't clear who, if anyone, besides the king, could give them permission or tell them what to do. The circumstances, some passengers may have thought, might offer the possibility of all sorts of liberties, including the Big One: to just do whatever they wanted. Some apparently felt so free that they suggested splitting from the main group and starting their own plantations, albeit with the same debt to the Adventurers and the same expectation of supplies and assistance.

We don't really know what was discussed on board the *Mayflower*, how vehemently anyone was suggesting a departure from the original plan, or what they may have wanted to do, but something was going on. Bradford later wrote of "discontented and mutinous speeches by some of the strangers among them suggested that when they came ashore they would use their own liberty, for none had power to command them, the patent they had being for Virginia and not for New England..."

The "strangers" he referred to were those not of the Separatist congregation, and maybe one of their rebellious voices was that of Stephen Hopkins, who'd been in a similar situation back in Bermuda — a shipwreck situation, but still a matter of a bunch of English people in a place they weren't supposed to be. When he plotted mutiny and suggested settling there instead of in Virginia, the governor sentenced him to death. He begged his way out of it, but had he learned his lesson? Now off the coast of New England in a ship that was supposed to be headed for Virginia, a ship in which no one had authority to sentence him to death, did he again suggest mutiny and unapproved settlement? Or did he share the legal advice he'd picked up on Devil's Isle? Did he think about his newborn son, Oceanus, and the wisdom of conformity?

A journalist noted the tensions.

> *The day before we came to harbor, observing some not well affected to unity and concord, but gave some appearance of faction, it was thought good there should be an association and agreement that we should combine together into one*

> *body, and to submit to such government and gov-*
> *ernors as we should by common consent agree to*
> *make and choose...*

In other words, the more responsible passengers — probably Separatists more than the strangers among them — came up with a mutinous idea of their own: that rather than abandon the civility and order that they had brought from England, they might establish their own government. They'd still be subjects of the king, but they'd elect their own leaders and make their own decisions. Their own government, they figured, "might be as firm as any patent."

Actually, the idea wasn't very mutinous at all. At most it qualified as just a bit uppity. It was the first time that a bunch of Europeans would just up and give themselves permission to start their own government. Between the lines of their self-decreed permission, one can almost hear timid whispers of *We, the people....* But they, the people (the male people, anyway) decided to be only so bold as to declare that they were taking the liberty to *choose* to bow to the king, the same who had wanted to jail them, even hang them, and still had the option of doing so. Between the lines of their self-decreed permission one can almost hear whispers of *We, the criminals on the lam....*

The document would not survive until America became a nation. *Mourt's Relation* and Bradford's *Of Plym-*

outh Plantation have copies of the wording, but nobody has
the original with the signatures. *Mourt's* author called it *an
association and agreement*. Bradford didn't call it anything.
It wasn't until after the American Revolution, more than a
century and a half later, that someone called it the Mayflower Compact.

It went like this:

> *We whose names are underwritten, the loyal
> subjects of our dread Sovereign Lord King James,
> by the Grace of God of Great Britain, France, and
> Ireland King, Defender of the Faith, etc.*
>
> *Having undertaken, for the Glory of God and
> advancement of the Christian Faith and Honour
> of our King and Country, a Voyage to plant the
> First Colony in the Northern Parts of Virginia,
> do by these presents solemnly and mutually in
> the presence of God and one of another, Covenant
> and Combine ourselves together into a Civil Body
> Politic, for our better ordering and preservation
> and furtherance of the ends aforesaid; and by vir-
> tue hereof to enact, constitute and frame such just
> and equal Laws, Ordinances, Acts, Constitutions
> and Offices, from time to time, as shall be thought
> most meet and convenient for the submission and*

obedience. In witness thereof we have hereunder subscribed our names at Cape Cod, the 11th of November, in the year of the reign of our Sovereign Lord King James, of England, France, Ireland the eighteenth, and of Scotland the fifty-fourth. Anno Domini 1620.

These are the men who signed the agreement:

John Carver, Edward Tilley, Degory Priest, William Bradford, John Tilley, Thomas Williams, Edward Winslow, Francis Cooke, Gilbert Winslow, William Brewster, Thomas Rogers, Edmund Margesson, Isaac Allerton, Thomas Tinker, Peter Brown, Myles Standish, John Rigsdale, Richard Britteridge, John Alden, Edward Fuller, George Soule, Samuel Fuller, John Turner, Richard Clarke, Christopher Martin, Francis Eaton, Richard Gardinar, William Mullins, James Chilton, John Allerton, William White, John Crackstone, Thomas English, Richard Warren, John Billington, Edward Doty, John Howland, Moses Fletcher, Edward Leister, Stephen Hopkins, and John Goodman.

It is supposed that those who did not sign were women or not yet twenty-one years of age. No one is known to have abstained for reasons of disagreement. The group was agreeing to settle together, write laws together, work together to pay off their common debt, and still answer to the same king from whom they had with such difficulty fled.

Having agreed on the compact, they "chose, or rather confirmed" John Carver as their governor for the next year. What, exactly, *governor* meant or what his powers were was not defined. Bradford wrote that Carver was a "godly man and well approved amongst them." Between the agreement on paper and the vague power entrusted to a single man, they had a government. Now they could move on.

Chapter Eight

The Discoveries

*M*ourt's Relation devotes many words to the weather. Few are the reports of pleasant conditions. Everyone was naturally inclined to keep an eye on the sky, the place where conditions of life and death came from. The settlers spent a good deal of their day and sometimes night exposed to the weather. It wasn't something they heard about in reports. They felt it on their skin and in their bones. It froze in their hair. It turned their cheeks a ruddy purple. It hurt their teeth. Back in England they had heard of the raw weather of New England, but they came unprepared for its actual chill and ferocity. They may have expected their southwestern route to lead them to a warmer clime.

Plymouth, England, is as close to the Arctic as the northern tip of Newfoundland. Plymouth, America, sits 700 miles closer to the equator. If logic applied to climate, Plymouth, America, on the 42nd parallel, should have been as balmy as Barcelona, Spain. Back in Leyden, in their discussions about whether to chance a move to America, it was argued that a hot climate would be a "noisome impediment" (i.e. annoying obstacle) that would not agree with their English bodies. New England, they figured, would offer a more comfortable climate.

But they couldn't have chosen a place of more noisome impediment. The coast of New England is assailed by three sources of cold: the prevailing westerly winds that have blown across a frozen continent, arctic cold fronts probing down from the north, and a cold arctic current flowing down the coast from Newfoundland. These three forces collide with the relatively warm, moist air flowing north over the Gulf Stream just a few miles out to sea. The collision stirs up an atmospheric battle. A clear, warm day can quickly turn windy and wet, the precipitation falling as warm rain, cold rain, frozen rain, sleet, or several consistencies of snow. Vast cyclones, spinning counterclockwise, float over the Gulf Stream. Though the storms move north, the winds curving around the northern edge of a cyclone come into New England from the northeast — the infamous nor'easters — lashing the coast with the kind of rain that explains why so many New Englanders live in Florida. The winds of a nor'easter can reach hurricane strength.

The winter weather makes Plymouth a poor place to live, even in the best of shelters. A winter in an unheated boat exposed to the wind had to be nothing less than excruciating. The *Mayflower* sat in water that in mid-November was probably dropping below 45 degrees. By late December it would drop below 40. The air would be chillier still, with breezes worsening the effects of cold on the human body. If the temperature inside the boat was above freezing, it wasn't much above and certainly was never, for even a moment, warm.

Even in mid-November, a person needs desperation and real faith in God to step thigh-deep into water like that. Because of shallow water, the ship could not come closer than three-quarters of a mile to shore. From there they could come closer to shore in the ship's longboat, but still they had to wade "a bow shot or two" into shore, that is, as far as a bow can shoot an arrow once or twice, that is, a couple of hundred yards. One can imagine the landing party inhaling the name of the Lord as they sank their legs into Cape Cod water. For many, these were the first steps toward not only religious freedom but also fatal illness. "Some did it necessarily, and some for their own pleasure," the journalist wrote, "but it brought to most, if not to all, coughs and colds, the weather proving suddenly cold and stormy, which afterwards turned to scurvy, whereof many died."

Scurvy may well have affected the passengers and crew, but scurvy is brought on not by cold but lack of vitamin C. After some five months of malnutrition, the scurbutic patient develops black-and-blue spots on the skin as capillaries break down and hemorrhage. The gums bleed. The teeth hurt as the roots rot. The breath stinks. The body aches. The spirit spirals into depression. But they had not been at sea for five months, and the journalist makes no mention of any symptoms unique to scurvy. Just coughs and colds, the symptoms of pneumonia, influenza, fever, all likely results of exposure.

The beer probably wasn't helping. Though it was a main source of hydration, especially during the crossing, and a good source of many nutrients, the alcohol robbed their bodies of other nutrients.

Their ailments could also have been what they called melancholy, what psychiatrists would later call depression. It could have been stress, and today a known cause of many ailments.

On November 11 (by the old calendar, or November 21 by the modern calendar), fifteen or sixteen men, well armed, made that first cold trip to shore. The ship had run out of firewood. There would be no hot food until they found fuel. In their wet and freezing clothes, they staggered up sandy hills that reminded them of Holland, "but much better." Beyond the sand they found "excellent black earth" as deep as the blade of a shovel, the equivalent of gold to anyone who plans to settle and plant. They wandered through an open forest of oak, pine, sassafras, juniper, birch, holly, ash, walnut. For their firewood they chose the juniper. It smelled sweet and strong, a gourmet heat much needed on an overcrowded ship of people who had not changed their clothes in six weeks.

Not that the passengers enjoyed much heat. The only heat they received on board came from each other, their livestock, or portions of the gruel du jour.

So when the men waded ashore or back to the boat, their breeches got wet and stayed wet. In fact, all the passengers spent the winter in clothes somewhere between damp and wet. They lived just a few feet above the ocean in conditions dank to an extreme. They might have made small fires in sandboxes on the ship, but the only place to build a large fire was on shore, and the only way to get on a shore was to wade.

Cold water didn't keep the women from an urgent necessity. On November 13, a Monday, first thing, the women came ashore and washed America's filthiest load of laundry.

The next project was to take ashore and reassemble the sections of the shallop. Its sections had been stored with the passengers on the gun deck. With this thirty-foot, single-mast, no-frills sail boat, they hoped to explore the coast and navigable rivers in search of a nice place to build a town, plant food, raise kids, worship God, and start a new civilization. But as they got the pieces laid out on the beach, they found the shallop "much opened with the people's lying in her" (according to *Mourt's Relation*), "much bruised and shattered in the ship with foul weather" (according to Bradford). The ship's carpenter informed the settlers that they wouldn't be going anywhere in a shallop for at least two weeks, maybe three. Neither Bradford nor Mourt's Relation tells us how many pieces or sections had to be fitted together or whether new planks had to be hewn and caulked and soaked. Such extensive repairs would have been excruciatingly difficult and all but impossible to finish in just two or three weeks. It's more likely, then, that the shallop had been transported in two sections: the fore and the aft. Like many such boats designed for transport on a ship, it had probably been built with two bulkheads at roughly the middle of the boat. The boat could then be sawed in half between the bulkheads, resulting in two water-tight sections. These sections could be later fastened tight to each other with screw, bolts, or pins. The repairs, then, were probably a relatively simple matter of tightening various fittings rather than replacing warped wood.

Impatience ruled. After sixty-eight days at sea, they did not want to wait two more weeks before looking for a place to settle. They also needed to find some food. They were under pressure from the ship's crew, too. Bradford wrote that it was "muttered by some" that if the passengers did not find a place soon, the crew wouldn't mind just dumping them and their measly goods on the beach so the ship could head for home before the worst of winter. Settlement wasn't a sailor's problem.

When they'd first sailed into the bay, they saw a river. If deep enough for a ship or even a boat, and if it flowed past fertile land, and if no one was shooting arrows from the underbrush, it might be the place to settle. And whether it was a nice river or not, the men certainly wouldn't mind taking a long hike on solid ground. Despite fear of Indians and the need to carry provisions on their backs instead of in the shallop, they prepared to explore a bit of their continent. Captain Myles Standish was to lead sixteen men, with William Bradford, Stephen Hopkins and Edward Tilley along for counsel and advice. Each man carried a matchlock musket and a sword. Some may have had left-handed daggers as well. Each man wore a steel vest over his torso and a steel helmet over his head. They may also have carried a few pikes and halberds. The pikes had steel points on fourteen-foot wooden poles. The halberts were about half that long, with sharp points extending beyond double axe blades. The pikes and halberds would be useful if the men had to charge an enemy line or to retreat under the charge of a cavalry. Neither battle tactic was likely. The Indians weren't so foolishly brave as to fight battles in an orderly line, and they had never seen a horse.

On Wednesday, November 15, they waded ashore and marched their wet breeches and soggy shoes single file along the shore. Unsure of what or whom they'd find, they probably hiked with lit matches, the long hemp cords they'd need to light the gunpowder of their muskets. Within a mile they saw their first Americans, just up the beach, five or six "savages" and their dog. The Americans took off into the woods but had to whistle to get their dog to follow. The English took off after them and followed their footprints for ten miles. Though the logic doesn't hold up too well, the journalist wrote that they "marched after them into the woods, lest other of the Indians should lie in ambush." It would seem more likely that by following the Indians, they'd rush into an ambush. Their approach would be no secret, with the sour smoke of their hemp matches blowing around, their boots tromping the ground, their steel vests clanking and screeching as they charged through the branches and brush.

When night closed in, they made a fire, posted three sentinels, and hunkered down for the night. If they felt the eyes of savages upon them, it probably wasn't just their imagination.

The English had yet to know what they meant when they said *savage*. They had yet to meet these people. *Savage* in those days referred simply to people who inhabited the forest and therefore lived outside the Christian-European culture. *Savage* has its roots in *sylvan*. As inhabitants of the dark forest, savages were, by definition, people unenlightened by the Christian love and good will that had illuminated civilization for over sixteen centuries, albeit with a dreadfully spotted record. The term *savage* did not exclude people who walked on the beach and whistled to their dogs, nor did it necessarily carry connotations of bloodthirst or violence. Still, the native Americans in the Cape Cod area had already given savages a bad name, though there's no doubt that the Christians were asking for trouble. During Champlain's trip through the area in 1605, the Nausets killed a sailor in a little battle over a kettle. When Champlain came back a year later, people remembered him. Several hundred ambushed a landing party, killing five. After the five were buried, the locals came back, dug up the bodies and killed them some more. The French evened things out by slaughtering half a dozen Indians just out of spite. When Master Thomas Dermer came along in 1619, it didn't matter that he had on board an Indian who had been to England and back, now working as a translator and guide. Irate Indians near Plymouth captured Dermer and probably would have introduced him to a gruesome death if his trusty Indian guide hadn't talked his compatriots into letting him go. But Dermer got no farther than the other side of the cape, an island the Wampanoag called Nope and which the English would later name Martha's Vineyard. There he got bushwhacked again, this time fatally.

Like most Europeans, the Separatists had heard only one side of a story that would have sounded quite different in a dialect of Algonquian. Relating the original decision to come to the New World, William Bradford wrote that his people feared what they'd heard about the savages.

> *[T]hose which should escape [disease] and or overcome these difficulties should yet be in continual danger of the savage people, who are cruel, barbarous and most treacherous, being most furious in their rage and merciless where they overcome* [i.e. overrun]*; not being content only to kill and take away life but delight to torment men in the most bloody manner that may be; flaying*

some alive with the shells of fishes, cutting off the
members and joints of others by piecemeal and
broiling on the coals, eat the collops of their flesh
in their sight whilst they live, with other cruelties
horrible to be related.

These were the people the English thought they were tracking down in hopes of preventing an ambush. The Americans probably had similar fears as they fled. At dawn the next morning, the English continued the chase. They came upon a long creek. They spotted the Indians again as they fled into the woods. The English kept after them, hoping to find Indian dwellings, but the fleeing savages had fled smart, forcing their pursers to charge into underbrush. The low, dense branches tore their armor to pieces and made the pikes and halberds impediments rather than weapons. With that, they changed their objectives. They didn't want savages; they wanted water. They were, as the journalist put it, "sore athirst," adrift in the underbrush with neither beer nor water, only biscuits, cheese, and, to ward off total sobriety, a little aquavitae. They marched down into a deep valley of brush and long grass. There they found sweet springs of fresh water, their first in North America. It was, in their thirst, as pleasant as beer or wine. They drank "with as much delight as ever we drunk drink in all our lives." Delivered from two months of seawater to such a source of sweet water, maybe they prayed: *He turneth the wilderness into a standing water, and dry ground into watersprings.*

From there they turned south to hit the beach. There, in accordance with a plan, they made a fire to signal the ship of their whereabouts. Then they turned again toward the river they had seen. In a valley they found a fine, clear pond of fresh water a musket shot wide, two musket shots long. Nearby they found fifty acres of cleared land all but pleading for a plow. In fact, they found evidence that Indians had planted the land in the past. A nice place to live? Maybe... except for the neighbors.

To not miss the river, they returned to the beach to follow the sea. Walking in the sand proved hard. Some of the men lagged behind. Bradford and others waited for them to catch up, then they all headed inland again.

They came to a little path and followed it to an eerie place with heaps of sand, one heap covered with mats. On the top they found a wooden thing, a mortar or something, sunk into the sand. An earthen pot was sunk at the end of the heap. With hands and swords they dug into the sand, soon uncovering a bow and then what seemed to be the rotted remains of arrows.

They were pretty sure they had themselves a gravesite and that if they dug more, they'd find more things. They wanted to learn more about the savages, to touch their exotic artifacts, maybe unearth their bones. They must have felt a confluence of conflicting feelings, a fear of nearby savages and the kind of hope that comes with knowing they were not alone in this new, harsh land. But they were pretty sure the local people, however unChristian they might be, wouldn't want their deceased disturbed, that *it would be odious unto them to ransack their sepulchers.* The Christians replaced the savage sand, left everything the way they'd found it, then moved on.

A little farther on, they found more corn stubble, this time of recent harvest. They found walnut trees laden with nuts. They found strawberry vines, grape vines, and then another field, and then another, and then another, bigger, and near it, the remains of an Indian house. Near the house, they found old planks of wood. They found a large kettle, apparently off a ship. They also found another heap of sand, but this one was newer than the other, with the prints of the savage hands that had patted it firm. They dug in and found a little basket full of fair Indian corn. They dug more and found a big, round basket, "cunningly made," narrow at the top, new and full of very fair corn of recent harvest. Besides kernels it held thirty-six ears of corn, some yellow, some red, others mixed with blue, a total of three or four bushels, as much as two men could lift.

This was big stuff, exactly what they needed for starter

seed. Indian corn was a native plant, sure to grow. They had brought none because England had none. *Corn* in England referred to just about any edible grass: Barleycorn was corn; wheat was corn. Indian corn — also called Indian wheat — was the stuff that grew on cobs, the perfect corn to plant in the land where it had grown. They could not have found a more valuable treasure.

While a few men stood guard, the rest dug and consulted. They decided that they needed the Indian corn more than the Indians did and that the Indians wouldn't mind if the new neighbors just borrowed the kettle for a while, just to carry the corn down to the beach. They'd return the kettle and pay for the corn as soon as they could find the rightful owners. They had no idea that, to the local people, corn wasn't just food. It was something sacred. It was also an irreplaceable stockpile for the winter. But the place seemed abandoned, and the needs of the Englishmen were great, so they stuffed their pockets and filled the kettle and hoisted it up on a staff for two men to carry. If they hadn't been so burdened with weapons and armor, they'd have taken more.

From the burglars' perspective, it was good that they'd dug up and carried away as much corn as they could. Within a few days, the ground was frozen solid and covered with snow. It would have been impossible to dig. Looking back on the larceny, Bradford attributed the timely find to God's goodness, "let His holy name have all the praise."

Nearby they found the ruins of a fort, a palisade of planks put up by Christians, they were sure. Not far from there they came out of the woods above two branches of a river that flowed around a high bank between them. The farther branch looked like it might be deep enough for a ship. It certainly was deep enough for canoes. A wooden dugout, rested on the near side, another on the far side. The explorers had no time to go down to see if the river was from inland or just a tidal inlet. They had to get back to the beach by the next day to signal their location with a fire. The people in the ship were expecting it.

They returned to the pond to set up camp for the night. There they lit a bonfire and built a barricade to keep the wind off, but it proved a very rainy night. The men took turns standing guard in the rain, their matches smoldering, their eyes peeled, waiting for someone to come see them about the corn, the kettle, and the graves.

The wet night put most of the muskets out of commission. Come morning, their matches soggy, their muskets no deadlier than clubs, they were less well armed than the people in the woods. All the English had for firepower were Standish's two flint-lock muskets. Flint-locks, or snaphances, didn't need the ember of a match, just the spark of a flint against steel. Still, statistically, one of the two flint-locks probably wouldn't fire. Given the moisture of the day, the other one probably wouldn't fire, either. With an urge to get their cold, wet bones back home before they caught an arrow, they sank the kettle in the pond and struck out in what seemed the right direction. But it wasn't. They soon lost their way. They came on a sapling bent over a strew-ing of acorns. Stephen Hopkins said it looked like a deer trap. William Bradford, bringing up the rear, didn't hear that theory in time. As he traipsed by, the tree snapped up and a noose snared his leg, no doubt to the joy of men who could use a good laugh.

It was an interesting noose, evidence of savage tech-nology. It looked as finely made as the rope of any roper in England. Good enough to keep. So they did.

Farther on they saw three bucks, three pairs of par-tridge, great flocks of wild geese and ducks, but if they managed to shoot any, the journalist of *Mourt's Relation* did not note it. They pressed on, through woods, over sand, into water up to their knees, until at last they saw the ship. They got their matches lit and fired off muskets to call attention. Soon Master Jones and several other people on shore came running. They decided to keep the corn for seed, and they vowed again to make good payment as soon as they could.

A few days later they made another excursion in search

of a place to live. The shallop was finally ready. Master Jones volunteered himself and ten sailors to take twenty-four explorers in the shallop and the ship's long boat to search for the river. Getting the long boat turned over, trussed up, off the deck, over the side and down to the water was a big chore that wouldn't be repeated often. Jones was doing them a favor.

The weather quickly turned rough. Both boats had to row to shore. Again, everyone had to wade to the beach. They marched six or seven miles in a stiff, cold wind. Snow blew down all day and night, dumping half a foot on the wet and unsheltered campers. "Some of our people that are dead," the journalist later wrote, "took the original of their death here."

The next day, the storm let up. The shallop came and took the men to the double-branched river they'd seen before. They called its mouth Cold Harbor. It was deep enough for the shallop but not for a ship. Several men, including Master Jones, tromped through the snow up the wider branch while the shallop followed. After four or five miles, Jones could hike no more. They resolved to spend the night under the protection of some pines. They shot three fat geese and six ducks for dinner. "We ate with soldiers' stomachs," the journalist wrote, "for we had eaten little that day."

They had planned to hike all the way to the headwaters of the river, but after that second night of sleeping in snow, they just didn't feel like it. They went back down to the river, where they found the canoe they'd seen before. They also saw some geese out in the water. As long as they had the canoe, it was worth a couple of potshots at the geese. They hit a couple, borrowed the canoe, and paddled out to get their kill. From there they ferried themselves across the river, seven or eight at a time. Then they returned to the place where they'd found the corn. They gave the place a name: Cornhill, possibly having in mind a place of the same name near London. They dug around some more, carving through the frozen ground with their cutlasses and swords and using levers to lift foot-thick chunks of earth. It was worth the effort. They found a bottle of oil, then more corn, then two or three baskets of corn, then a bag of beans, then more corn. Master Jones warned them of more bad weather coming, but the others wanted to keep digging. They sent Jones down to the shallop with the weak, the sick, and the corn, asked him to come back with mattocks and spades. Eighteen men spent yet another night on the cold, hard ground.

The next day they wandered up and down paths in hopes of finding an Indian village. For a while they found no signs of people, but then they came to another heap of sand, this one bigger than the others. They dug in, found a mat and under it a bow, and under the bow another mat, then a board finely carved and painted, and under it, another mat, and under the mat, two bundles, one large, one small. They opened the larger one and found a fine red powder and the bones and skull of a man...a man with yellow hair. Among his bones were a knife, a needle, some old iron things, and a pair of breeches. It was the corpse of a European.

They opened the smaller bundle, found the same flour-fine powder, a little bow, some knick-knacks, and the bones and skull of a child. Its legs were bound up in string and bracelets with fine white beads.

They kept a few items and covered up the rest. Then the theories started. Maybe it was an Indian king and his child. But the yellow hair and maybe the breeches indicated someone of the Christian persuasion, perhaps some respected European who had died among Indian friends and been buried with all due honor. Or maybe he was killed by the Indians and buried in some savage rite of triumph. *Savage* was yet to be defined. They weren't even sure whether savages wore breeches.

Meanwhile, down near the beach, two of Jones's sailors spotted two low, domed houses in the woods. The sailors had muskets, and they saw no one around, so they poked in, grabbed a few things, and went to find Bradford and the

rest. Seven or eight men came to investigate. The journalist described the houses as made of long saplings bent into
arches with each end stuck in the ground. Well woven mats
covered the poles down to the ground. The door was just a
yard high and covered with a mat. Inside a man could stand.
The walls had another layer of mats on the inside. In the
center were the charred remains of a cookfire. Four stakes
stood around it to hold sticks for hanging pots. The roof had
a hole in the center, right over the fireplace. The hole could
be covered by a mat that hung from a pole leaned against
the outside of the house. Around the fire lay bed matting.
The home still had its utensils — wooden bowls, trays, and
dishes, earthen pots, crab shells, hand baskets, and, most
interestingly, an English bucket missing its handle. They
found cut lengths of sedge and bulrushes for making mats.
They found food: parched acorns, pieces of fish, a broiled
herring, seeds of tobacco and plants unknown. They found
signs of a hunt: eagle claws, the horns of a hart, several
deer hooves and three deer heads, one still fresh. People
were not long out of this house. Kindly Christian larcenists
that they were, they helped themselves to only a few items
of interest, regretting that they had only beads to leave as a
sign of peace. They told themselves they would settle with
the Indians as soon as they met.

Chapter Nine

Cold December

The discovery of such cozy, lived-in abodes got the settlers thinking a little harder about building homes for themselves. Three months in the cramped, cold, common quarters in the bowels of the *Mayflower* was enough — almost six months if they included the weeks in transit from Leyden to Southampton and the two false starts with the *Speedwell*. Some pilgrims had had it with the pilgrimage. Cold Harbor, some argued, wasn't so bad. If nothing else, it was *right there*. They could start moving *right then, that day*. No more sailing around in frozen clothes, no more risking the shallop to winter squalls, no more tromping through the snow, no more waiting for Indian arrows, no more sleeping wherever they happened to poop out. The river provided a reasonably good harbor even if not for ocean-going ships. It was a nice spot, "healthful, secure, and defensible." It had freshwater ponds. The stubble in the fields proved the land was suitable for corn. The bay was good for fishing, even whaling. In fact, the whales here were perfectly stupid, coming right alongside the ship without fear. One had floated for a long time just half a musket-shot away. Just to see what would happen, one man took a shot at it. His musket, lock, stock and barrel, blew up in his face. The whale then gave a snuff and swam away. But there would be more, and apparently they'd be easy to harpoon, if they'd had harpoons, which they didn't. But if they had — and they might, as soon as the *Mayflower* returned to England and a supply ship came back with supplies — they'd have access to oil, which meant not only light but revenue.

   The journalist wrote: *But the last and especial reason was, that now the heart of winter and unseasonable weather was come upon us, so that we could not go upon coasting and discovery without danger of losing men and boat, upon which would follow the overthrow of all, especially considering what variable winds and sudden storm do there arise. Also, cold and wet lodging had so tainted our people, for scarce any of us were free from vehement coughs, as if they should continue long in that estate it would endanger the lives of many, and breed diseases and infection among us. Again, we had yet some beer, butter, flesh, and other such victuals left, which would quickly be all gone, and then we should have nothing to comfort us in the great labor and toil we were like to undergo at the first. It was also conceived, whilst we had competent victuals, that the ship would stay with us, but when that grew low, they would be gone and let us shift as we could.*

Others saw no reason to rush. They had a whole continent to themselves. Why take the first place they came to? They'd heard about a place called Anguum or Angoum some twenty leagues — sixty miles — to the north. According to the vague maps of early explorers, Anguum had an excellent harbor, better ground, better fishing, and, for all anyone knew, a better place to settle for good. It might offer a body of water more along the lines of a lake than the ponds above Cold Harbor, which for all anyone knew would dry up in summer.

After all due discussion, it was decided that it wouldn't hurt to do a little more exploring around Cape Cod Bay. Robert Coppin, the ship's pilot and second mate, said he knew of a great navigable river where the cape met the continent, just eight leagues away. He'd been there before, trading with Indians. He remembered the place well. They called it Thievish Harbor because some Indians had stolen a harpoon.

On December 4, a young man named Edward Thompson, servant of William White, passed on. Nothing else is known of him except that, as he had not signed the Association and Agreement, he was most likely under twenty-one.

That same day, the men organized a "discovery" party to take the shallop to Thievish Harbor. They tried to leave on the next day, December 5, but the weather resisted.

Meanwhile, back at the *Mayflower*, one of the Billington boys got hold of some gunpowder and shot and decided to make some "squibs" — firecrackers — in his family's little cabin. The young fool had powder, shot, flints, and iron things within an arm's length of half a barrel of gunpowder, a charged fowling piece, and some kind of small cooking or heating fire. For reasons unknown, the fowling piece discharged, hurling sparks all over the place. One spark in the barrel would have put the *Mayflower* out of its misery, but by a miracle attributed to God, no one was hurt.

On December 6, after a busy day of preparing the shallop and its equipment, twenty men — Separatists Carver,

Bradford, Winslow, John Tilley, his brother Edward, and John Howland; their security man Standish; Strangers Richard Warren, Stephen Hopkins, and Edward Doty; seamen John Allerton and Thomas English; Master's mates Clark and Coppin, three sailors and the master gunner — set off for Thievish Harbor. The journalist described the weather as rainy and cold. It took them the rest of that day and all that night to row around the shallow water of a sandy point. Once they got around the point, they hoisted the sail. But then Edward Tilley took ill. So did the master gunner, but the expedition kept going. The sailing got easier the next day as they hugged the shore, but sea spray froze on their clothes like iron. It probably felt as heavy as iron, too, as spray hit them and froze, adding layers that never drained away. As night drew on, they headed into the shore of a wide bay. As they came in, they saw ten or twelve Indians very busy with something big and black. When the Indians spotted the shallop, they ran to and fro, picking up and making off with whatever they'd been working on. With difficulty the shallop made its way around sandbars and came in close to shore. From there they waded in. In wet breeches and frozen shirts, they pulled together a barricade, started a fire, and set out sentinels for the night. They saw the smoke of the Indian fire four or five miles farther down the beach.

Back at the *Mayflower*, Jasper More, the second oldest

of the four young Mores, the one being raised by John and Katherine Carver, died. He was seven.

The next morning the explorers divided up, eight men to the shallop, the rest to follow the shore in hopes of finding a river feeding into the bay. They found no river, but the water near shore was a good five fathoms deep, enough for a ship. Above the beach they found a level area, but it wasn't growing much. They found fresh water running in two creeks, the first running fresh water they'd seen since arriving. They also found a pilot whale — they called it a grampus — five or six paces long, dead on the sand. The shallop spotted two more dead under the water. Apparently they'd run aground and been pinned by frost and ice. It was a good place to call Grampus Bay. Had the men brought the right equipment, they might have tapped the thick blubber for oil. Some of the blubber was two inches thick.

Farther down the beach they found a grampus that the Indians had been cutting up into long slices. The men followed prints of bare feet until they disappeared into the woods. Someone spotted Indians among the trees, and the party took off after them. They followed a path, passing old corn fields until they came to a burial site surrounded by a palisade of spires four or five yards tall, like a fence around a churchyard cemetery. Some of the graves had their own palisades. It reminded them of the graves at the place they'd named Cornhill, but, in the journalist's words, "more sumptuous." Some even had the remains of Indian houses over them, their arched ribs stripped of mats. Less respectful then they had been at Cornhill, perhaps more desperate for food or clues about American life, the men dug up a few graves, had a look and moved on. They passed more old corn fields. They passed houses that had been lately dwelled in but now lacked their mat coverings. They found buried baskets, hoped to find them full of corn, but they held only parched acorn. They saw no people.

The sun was dropping low, the air taking on the chill of a late December afternoon. They headed out to the beach, saw the shallop rather far off. As it approached, they prepared a campsite, gathered firewood, ate the rest of their small supply of food, posted guards and settled into the sand to sleep until, about midnight, a great and hideous cry pierced their sleep. The sentinels screamed "Arm! Arm!" Someone shot off a couple of muskets, probably just aiming into the dark of woods to bolster the little fort with a good chunk of noise. The cry ceased. One of the sailors said he had heard such a noise in Newfoundland. He supposed it the howl of wolves or something. Whatever it was, it let the men go back to sleep.

They awoke at about five o'clock, just as the eastern horizon lightened a bit. They tested their muskets, said their prayers, perhaps finding relevance in Psalm 106, *Save us, O LORD our God, and gather us from among the heathen, to give thanks unto thy holy name, [and] to triumph in thy praise.* That said, they started gathering their things to carry down to the shallop. There was some discussion about whether to carry their arms and wear their armor on each trip. Some said they should be prepared. Others figured they could make the short trip quickly enough, and far more easily, if they weren't lugging muskets, swords, and leather corsets. They hauled stuff down to water's edge, some leaving their weaponry there, others leaving their arms at the campsite. The men were just going back up for breakfast when again the wolf howls shot through the camp. But this time the notes were different, and a sentinel came running into camp, crying, *"They are men! Indians! Indians!"* Arrows followed him. The men dashed for their weapons. Myles Standish had his snaphance on hand — the only gun in the party that could be discharged without a match. For the sake of a good, strong boom, he let off a shot aimed at nothing but the dark of the primeval forest. Someone else managed to get off a musket shot. By then, two other muskets were up and ready, matches lit. Standish told them to hold fire until they had something to aim at. They would have only four shots to counter the innumerable savages that were launching the rain of arrows. In the time it took to reload, the Indians could charge in and put arrows through all of them. The English prepared to deliver those four precious shots through the open side of the barricade. If the attackers came through that side, there would be no way out through the barricade of sticks and branches behind them. Worried that the shallop not be defended, they called down to the men on the beach. The men called back that they were uninjured and hollered, *"Be of courage!"* Three shots exploded from the beach, and men shouted for coals to light the matches. Someone in the campsite heaved a burning log to his shoulder and hurried to the beach. The enemy did not appear, but the arrows kept sailing in and the howling continued. The journalist described the sound as *Whoach woach ha ha hach woach.*

The men couldn't see much in the early dawn light of the forest, but they themselves stood out in the light of their own fire. They did spot "a lusty man" loosing arrows from behind a tree just half a musket-shot away. His arrows came from far enough away that the men were able to duck under them. They shot back at him three times but missed. Someone took careful aim for the killshot, hit the tree beside the man's head, blasting him with bark and splinters. He screamed and retreated into the woods. The English took off in hot pursuit. Before they went too far, they stopped. At Standish's signal, they shouted in unison and shot off a couple of muskets just to show that they were neither afraid nor discouraged.

Back at the campsite, they found eighteen arrows and guessed that many more might be found under the leaves on the ground. Some had tips of brass, others of hart horn or eagle claw. The arrows had hit no one, but some coats hanging on the barricade were shot through and through. The journalist, no doubt imagining himself wearing one of those coats, saw divine providence working to the Christian favor. "Thus it pleased God to vanquish our enemies and give us deliverance," he wrote. "By their noise we could not guess that they were less than thirty or forty, though some thought that they were many more."

They prayed thanks for their deliverance — perhaps a psalm: *Thou has rebuked the heathen....* then named the place The First Encounter, got into their shallop and sailed for Thievish Harbor.

Meanwhile, back at the ship, another deliverance was taking place. Susanna White, wife of William, mother of Resolved, gave birth to a boy. They named him Peregrine, a Latin word meaning pilgrim.

Then, on December 8, James Chilton died. He left a wife and a thirteen-year-old daughter on the *Mayflower* and more offspring back in England and Leyden. He was sixty-four.

The shallop sailed west along the cape and curved north along the mainland, moving at good clip through a cold curtain of rain and snow. They saw neither river nor creek worth exploring but covered fifteen leagues before the weather turned rough — good progress they should have known better than to trust. The waves battered the stern so hard that the hinges on the rudder broke. Two men grabbed oars and fought the growing waves as night drew on. The journalist wrote that they were "much troubled and in great danger," but Master Coppin bade them be of good cheer. Through the storm he saw the harbor he'd remembered from years ago. To pull in, they opened the sail, steered as best they could with the oars until the gale snapped the mast in three pieces. Bradford wrote little of their fear as they struggled against the waves, no rudder, no sail, clothes frozen stiff, teeth clattering, bodies cold to the bone, no one in the world having any idea where they were...no one but God, Who, as Bradford relates it, sent them a strong tide flooding into the harbor.

Except now, closer in, Coppin, peering through the rain, snow, and dim light, said he'd never seen the place before. He didn't know it, but rather than looking into the harbor, he was looking between two fingers of land that extended south across the upper half of the harbor. The finger closest to the ocean, known today as the Gurnet, was a reef frothing with waves. The inner finger, called Saquish, seemed to be the continent itself. It just didn't look like the place he knew, but it was too late to do anything about it. Their long, agonizing journey was about to end in disaster. Copin begged God's mercy for his mistake as the rudderless, sailless boat drifted toward the thundering white breakers. As they drifted helplessly toward their death, some may have fortified themselves with a psalm: *They reel to and fro, and stagger like a drunken man, and are at their wits' end. When their art and means fail them, they are compelled to confess that only God's providence preserves them. Then are they glad because they be quiet; so he bringeth them unto their desired haven.*

It was too soon to give up this pilgrimage. God had not sent them there to drown in the dark. A strong seaman manhandled an oar as a rudder to help God get the boat turned around. They rowed into the cold, rainy night, desperate for somewhere, anywhere, to rest. The ship was leagues away, the continent impossible to reach, the sea black, heaving and, for all they could tell, as infinite as the universe. After all they'd been through, after coming so far, they were just one wave from death. If they disappeared, the ship would be without mates, the passengers without their strongest men. "It was dark and rained sore," Bradford wrote, "yet in the end they got under the lee of a small island and remained there all that night in safety." They named the place Clark's Island, perhaps because Master's Mate John Clark was in the boat and had helped guide it through the cold, dark, windy night to shore.

They debated whether to stay in the boat, for fear of Indians, or go onto the island to make a fire. Some stayed; some went. With much ado they got wet wood to burn, and soon the men in the boat decided that warmth was worth the risk of Indians. "After midnight, Bradford wrote, "the wind shifted to the northwest and it froze hard.

"But though this had been a day and night of much trouble and danger unto them, yet God gave them a morning of comfort and refreshing (as usually He doth to His children) for the next day was a fair, sunshining day, and they found themselves to be on an island and secure from Indians, where they might dry their clothes, fix their weapons and rest themselves; and gave God thanks for His mercies in their manifold deliverances."

They spent that day, Saturday, December 9, building a shelter. The next day, the Sabbath, they rested.

On Monday they explored the harbor. It was just a little tricky to get in around a reef. They lowered weights into the water and found it deep enough to bring the *Mayflower* within a mile and a half of land — close enough for an easy row into shore.

On this date, December 11, the landing party may or may not have eased the shallop up to a certain rock near the mouth of a brook. The rock itself was a pilgrim, an arrival from somewhere else. No other rocks of similar composition have been found in Plymouth. A glacier may have brought it from the north. Judging by its components, it looks like it might be from ledge of Dedham granodiorite from the Boston area. Millennia of waves may have nudged it up from deep in the sea. Six hundred million years before that, it was a liquid a mile or more below the surface of the earth. It may have come to the surface during the Paleozoic Era, when all of Earth's land formed a single giant continent called Pangaea. When Pangaea split apart, the Atlantic Ocean opened between Europe and North America. Geologists believe that the area of North America's Plymouth was once attached to the area that became the British Isles. Plymouth Rock may be the very distant cousin of a rock in England. If poets ruled the earth, its other half would be in the other Plymouth.

But we do not know where, exactly, the shallop pulled up at Plymouth on that first day. It could have been anywhere along the beach within the protective arm of land that reached into the harbor. If logic applies, the men would have looked for a place where they could get out of the boat without sinking their legs into winter seawater. The water at the mouth of the brook may have been deep enough to bring the shallop in close to land. The rock, which was much bigger than it is today and quite likely in a different spot, may have extended into the water just far enough for the shallop to reach it. Such a rock at such a spot would have been a perfect place to get out of a boat. It's not impossible that Pilgrim feet really did step onto Plymouth Rock. But the first foot was definitely not that of the mythologized and unnamed young woman whose sole and toes were pure enough to bless the new continent. More likely it was a man in wet clothes with a musket or an ax in his hand. Whoever it was, he would have been glad to step directly from the boat onto something solid and dry. No one, however, left a written record of stepping onto a rock.

Nor did they meet the friendly band of noble Indians so often depicted in paintings of this historic event. But they certainly were on the look-out for Indians. Had there been a welcoming party, somebody might have killed somebody, and the history of America would have started in a different direction.

The men explored the mainland, found cornfields and brooks of fresh water, "a place very good for situation." It was definitely worth a closer look.

They returned to *Mayflower* with the good news that they had found a place to live.

138

The news, the journalist wrote, did much comfort their hearts. But they had bad news for the heart of William Bradford. The day after they'd left on their exploration, his wife, Dorothy, had fallen off the ship and drowned. She was twenty-three. She left not only her husband William but her son, John, just three years old, still back in Leyden, waiting for his parents to make America safe for him.

Mourt's Relation does not mention the event (nor most other deaths). Despite any evidence of what actually happened, people have long wondered whether maybe Dorothy jumped rather than fell. Such thoughts are based on conjecture, sympathetic imaginations conjuring up the emotions of a young woman under excruciating pressure. Dorothy hadn't seen her only son in over four months, and a seven-year-old child had just died a few feet away from her. Six weeks after arriving at the land of her new home, she was stuck in a cold, fetid, overcrowded ship. The interpersonal relationships below deck could not possibly have been easy. The shore of Cape Cod in November offered a bleak future. Her husband had just left her alone for the third time in a month as he continued a venture that just didn't look like it was going to work out. She was cold, day and night. She hadn't had a decent meal in months. She may well have been suffering from scurvy, a cause of not only pain but depression.

But the weather was as bad at the *Mayflower* as it had been at the shallop. The ship was rolling, the deck wet, maybe even icy, and Dorothy may well have been weak and unsteady with illness. She was the mother of a son, and she had a kind and loving husband. She believed in a God who loved her, and she feared a Hell for those who sinned. Whether she jumped in despair or slipped from a frozen deck, even the people on the *Mayflower* may not have known for sure.

On Thursday, December 15 they weighed anchor and sailed for Thievish Harbor. The wind cooperated briefly but then changed, forcing the ship to drop anchor two leagues short of the harbor. There they rested until the winds changed again, which they soon did, but just long enough for them to slip into the harbor. Half an hour later, the winds were blowing back toward Cape Cod, but by that time, their anchor had dug into the sand in the lee of the place that Master John Smith Master had visited in 1614 and which Prince Charles later named Plimouth and which the passengers of the *Mayflower* would for the next few months refer to only as *the place we discovered*.

Samuel de Champlain had been there, too, in 1605. He ducked into the harbor to get out of the wind but ran aground on a sandbar. With nothing else to do until the tide came in, he sketched a quick map. It shows depths in the harbor, including the shallow one under his ship. It shows drawings of sand dunes, forests, a man with a bow, and eight houses beside corn fields. He called the place Port du Cap St. Louis. He reported friendly natives in canoes and hemp growing five feet tall.

The ancestors of those natives may have seen Norwegians row by in 1010 or thereabouts. Others may have seen John Cabot sail by in 1498. They may have met a Portuguese castaway, Miguel Cortereal, who may have lived among natives in the area from 1502 until 1511. (A forty-ton rock at the mouth of the Taunton River, around the other side of the Cape, seems to have inscribed in it "Miguel Cortereal by will of God, here Chief of the Indians," along with what may be the date 1511 and a Portuguese coat-of-arms — either that or Algonquin pictures or Norwegian runes.) Giovanni da Verrazano explored the area in 1524 and saw houses just like the ones the *Mayflower* discoverers were finding, except people still lived in them. In 1602, Bartholomew Gosnold and 32 sailors harvested sassafras and cedar somewhere around there. They also saw a lot of fish and named the place Cape Cod. Nine months later, the pilot from the Gosnold voyage, Martin Pring, returned with two ships, the *Speedwell* (no relation to *Mayflower's* leaky cohort) and the *Discoverer*. He sailed into a harbor with a channel that winded like a snail shell, twenty fathoms deep at the entrance, seven in a landlocked anchorage near a pleasant hill and sassafras all around — maybe a cove near the tip of Cape Cod, maybe Plymouth Bay itself. He called it Whitson Bay. His men built a hut on the hill, traded trinkets for a birch bark canoe, or maybe just stole it, then sawed up some sassafras, loaded it into their ship and sailed home. In 1609, Henry Hudson stopped by Cape Cod on his way to Manhattan. Samuel Argall came around in 1610, searching for cod to feed the people of Jamestown. In 1611, Edward Harlow's ship dropped anchor near Cape Cod, got into a fight with some local people. They attacked his ship with canoes, swiped a dingy, took it to shore, filled it with sand. Harlow forgot what he'd come for, captured five natives instead, one of them named Epenow, and took them to England. In 1614, Dutchman Adrian Block, whose ship had burned at Manhattan, test-sailed a jury-rigged yacht up Long Island Sound to Cape Cod, claiming land as Nieu Nederlant as he went. He drew a map of a bay he called Cranes. It looked very much like a place that Champlain had mapped, and it's quite possible the Separatists had seen this Dutch map before they left Leyden.

John Smith also passed through in 1614, and his evil partner, Thomas Hunt, came along a short while later. Smith made maps and bought beaver pelts. Hunt kidnapped several Nausets and Patuxets and sold them in Spain. When

Nicholas Hobson came along later that year, led by the same Epenow that Harlow had captured, he found hostile people near Nantucket. Apparently Hunt had taught them all they needed to know about white people in big ships. Epenow escaped, and Hobson sailed home with an empty hold.

Five years later, along came Master Thomas Dermer. A year later, he came back again. Of all the places he'd seen in New England, Plymouth Harbor was about the best. Six months before the arrival of the *Mayflower*, he wrote:

"I would that the first plantation might here be seated, if there come to the number of fifty persons, or upward. Otherwise Charlton [the Charles River, near Boston], because there the savages are less to be feared. The Pokanokets, which live to the west of Plymouth, bear an inveterate malice to the English, and are of more strength than all the savages from thence to Penobscot [Maine]....The soil of the borders of this great bay may be compared to most of the plantations I have seen in Virginia. The land is of divers sorts, for Patuxet is a hardy but strong soil; Nauset and Patuxet are for the most part a blackish and deep mould much like that where groweth the best tobacco in Virginia. In the bottom of that great bay is store of cod and bass or mullet, etc. But above all he commends Pokanoket for the richest soil, and much open ground fit for English grain, etc."

That said, he sailed around the coast and down to Martha's Vineyard, where he met up with Epenow and his friends. They were still mad about Harlow and Hunt. They shot Thomas Dermer with arrows, wounding him and killing several of his men. Dermer headed for Virginia but soon died of his arrow wounds.

The Pilgrims probably knew of neither Dermer's recommendation nor his death, but from the deck of the *Mayflower* they knew they liked the place. The harbor was compassed with goodly land, and the bay had two islands covered with oak, pine, walnut, beech, sassafras, grape vines, and trees of types they had yet to name. The journalist reported a harbor shaped like a sickle or a fishhook. Was it his subconscious or a poetic flair that saw the harbor as a tool for producing food?

On Monday, December 18, they went ashore. They found mussels, an easy meal readily plucked from shallow water. They saw innumerable "excellent good fowl." The journalist wrote that it was "a hopeful place," and in his hopes he saw skate, cod and flatfish that weren't exactly there but would be, he was sure, in their season. He saw crabs and lobster that would be, "in their time infinite." They found Indian corn fields, soil black and fat, brooks of sweet fresh water. They walked among noble woods: ash for fires, walnut for nuts, gun stocks, oak for clapboards and houses (and acorns for pigs), beech for building, sassafras for medicinal tea and export, birch, hazel, holly, and ash for all sorts of things. They found cherry trees. Plum trees. Wild grape. Despite the weeks of frost, they found green herbs: strawberry leaves, sorrel, yarrow, carvel, brooklime, liverwort, watercress. They found onion and leeks, flax and hemp. They found the stuff they needed to sustain their lives, not an Eden but a nice place to build one. The journalist didn't see a dreary landscape glazed with snow and drizzled with sleet off the North Atlantic. He saw potential.

> *Here is sand, gravel and excellent clay, no better in the world, excellent for pots, and will wash like soap, and great store of stone, though somewhat soft, and the best water that ever we drank, and the brooks now begin to be full of fish.*

They made quick for the ship, reported their find, and then slept the good sleep of the dead-tired. On Tuesday, December 19, they took the shallop up a very pleasant river which at high tide could float a ship but at low tide could barely keep the shallop off the bottom. They went three miles upstream, saw some nice places to plant but deemed them too far from the sea, where they planned to spend a lot of time fishing for food and profit. Given the likelihood of savages along the way, it would be a bad commute. Besides, the woods were too thick for so few to clear. They decided to settle the place later, after they had a stronger population.

Back at the bay, they checked out an island, figuring it would be easy to defend, but it was too rocky, too cold for corn, and for drinking water had nothing but puddles. They went back to the *Mayflower* to discuss. They called on God for direction. God said *location, location, location.* Their victuals nearly spent, their beer to the bottom of the barrel, real winter just getting underway, they resolved to explore no more. They narrowed the choices to one of the two on the mainland. They liked the area near the hill the most. It had old Indian corn fields already cleared, the sweet brook that would soon be filled with fish, the many delicate springs, the harbor, the commanding hill where they could mount their ordnance, the view of the bay. Within the harbor, an arm of land reached out as if to shelter the place where the brook met the sea. It was a cove within a harbor within a bay, a place that just plain felt safe. The firewood was a little far off, and for all they knew, it was Indian land, but yes, that was the place. Come morning they would go ashore and begin to build houses.

Chapter Ten

The Great Dying

On Wednesday, December 20 (or December 30 in the modern calendar), several men went ashore to scout around for the best place to settle. The weather gave them a classic New England welcome. Cold wind sliced at them, and a bone-chilling rain dug into their clothes. These were the atmospheric conditions for which New Englanders still reserve the word *miserable*. Despite the weather, they hunkered down, built some kind of lean-to or windbreak, maybe got a fire going, maybe not. They sent the shallop back to the ship with instructions to bring more people in the morning so they could start building houses. But during the night, the weather grew worse. The landing party spent the night in wind and rain, hoping that come morning the shallop would return with food, tools, and help.

But December 21 was as bad as December 20. Not until 11:00 that morning did the shallop manage to go in to shore with some food. It may also have carried the body of Richard Britteridge, who had just died. We do not know whether he was married or had children. No one on the *Mayflower* shared his name. We do not know how old he was or why he had wanted to move to America. He signed the Planter's Association and Agreement and six weeks later passed away. We do not know where they buried him except that it was probably in a shallow, unmarked grave of sand.

Wind kept the shallop on shore for a second night of cold, wet misery. Friday, December 22, dawned as nastily as the two days before. Again the shallop would not sail. The people on shore were stuck there, the people on board unable to do much more than hold on. Mary Allerton, wife of Isaac, mother of Bartholomew, Remember, and Mary, went into labor. She had buried an unnamed child in Leyden, and now, as the *Mayflower* rocked in the waves and swung around on her anchor, Mrs. Allerton delivered another child, a son, but again born without life.

Saturday, December 23, all who could went ashore to fell and drag trees to be sawed up into lumber and timber for building.

Sunday, December 24. On this day Solomon Prower, stepson of the scornful Christopher Martin, former governor of the *Mayflower*, died. The others rested for the Sabbath. But not completely. Savages in the forest, ignorant of the day, hooted and howled. The Christians prepared to repel an assault, but nothing came from the dark of the woods besides the ferocious ululations.

Monday, December 25, all men worked, felling trees, sawing them into sections and planks, carrying them out of the forest. They collected fresh water for the ship. Again, howls from the woods sent them scurrying for muskets, but again, no attack. Twenty men stayed on shore that night. Those on board shared a bit of the dwindling supply of beer. The Separatists made no celebration for the birth of their Savior. To do so would have been presumptuous, idolatrous, papally sacrilegious and in no way Biblical, for the Good Book makes no mention of parties for the birthday of God's son. It doesn't even say when that day is. The beer was probably a Christmas gesture of Master Jones. The Separatists would have accepted it not in celebration nor communion but simply because it was good. Those on shore slept in a storm of wind and rain without benefit of beer.

Tuesday, December 26: rain, wind, cold.

Wednesday, December 27: back to work.

Thursday, December 28: They assume a street running east and west from the beach to a hill, which they called the Mount, that rose 120 feet above sea level. They plan a "high way" that runs south from the street to a clear, shallow brook. The street and highway would lead to three gates in the palisade that would surround the town. Eventually, the governor's house would stand at the only intersection in town. Each house got a lot half a pole wide and three in length — eight feet three inches by forty-nine feet six inches — for each person in the household. Each lot would have its own garden and a fence of sharpened poles. To expedite the building of shelter, men with no wives were assigned to the homes of families. The first living quarters on land wouldn't be much roomier than the gun deck of the *Mayflower*.

They wanted this business out of the way, shelter built as soon as possible because despite the grace of God, they were not surviving well. The journalist wrote that they were "growing ill with cold, for our former discoveries" [i.e. explorations] "in frost and storms, and the wading at Cape Cod, had brought much weakness amongst us, which increased so every day more and more, and after was the cause of many of their deaths." In other words, the cold was killing them.

Friday, December 29: rainy, windy, cold.

Saturday, December 30: rainy, windy, cold. In the distance, smoke.

Monday, January 1: The journalist complains that because of the shallow harbor, the *Mayflower* must stay a mile and a half from shore. Trips in the shallop are hindered by the tides. The journalist makes no note of the new year because it is still almost three months off. By their calendar, 1621 starts on the Feast of the Assumption, March 25.

Wednesday, January 3: People gathering thatch around corn fields see the smoke of great fires in the distance. They see no savages, but they know they are out there and are burning something.

Thursday, January 4: Myles Standish and a contingent of four or five men go to look for the fires and the Indians. They find houses, but they have not been lately inhabited. They shoot an eagle, bring it home for dinner. It tastes just like mutton.

Friday, January 5: A sailor finds a live herring on the beach. The sailor gives the fish to Master Jones for his supper. The passengers are given nothing but hope; maybe a season of fish is arriving. The herring is the second fish anyone has caught in two months. The other was a cod. The problem: no small fishhooks.

Saturday, January 6: Christopher Martin takes ill on board the ship.

Sunday, January 7: They rest. Christopher Martin doesn't look good. No doubt he's thinking about his stepson, who died just two weeks ago, not to mention poor Billy Butten, little Jasper More, James Chilton, and Richard Bitteridge, all found cold in their beds just a few feet from where Martin lies. He no doubt saw them lifted from the ship and lowered to the shallop, rowed to shore and buried in the sand. Governor Carver comes back from shore to speak with Martin about his will.

Monday, January 8: The day starts off sunny. Master Jones takes the shallop in search of fish. They don't get far before they hit a storm, but they kill three large seals and an "excellent good" cod, giving them hope that fish are coming into season. They need it. Food is short, and they're running out of beer.

On this day Christopher Martin follows his stepson into the hereafter and a shallow grave in the sand. He leaves his wife, Mary, but not for long.

From shore, good news. Young Francis Billington, the same young fool who shot off a musket next to a powder keg in a small cabin on the most important ship in the world, unwitting ancestor of President James Garfield, has redeemed himself. He has climbed a hill and there climbed a tree. From there he cast his eyes to the west, where he spotted the Pacific Ocean. Or some other great sea. Has the elusive

Northwest Passage been found? In need of expert confirmation, he takes a ship's mate to verify. The great sea, it turns out, consists of two lakes, one five or six miles around, the other about half that size. A brook drained the larger lake, the same Town Brook that ran through Plymouth and past a certain big rock on the beach. The lakes weren't as good as the Pacific Ocean, but they were a fine source of fresh water and lots of fish and waterfowl. They came to name one of the lakes Fresh Lake, but later it becomes known as Billington's Sea. The smaller is still called Little Pond.

While up at the lakes, Billington and his friend also came across seven or eight Indian houses. The proximity to savages scared them. They'd brought only one musket — just one shot, one boom to hold off any assault from the village. But they found the same eerie, inexplicable situation they had always found: habitations without inhabitants.

Meanwhile, the settlers were still inhabitants without habitation. While private land ownership was their long-term goal, they had to get there by way of temporary communism — a common house where those on shore could stay with reasonable comfort and safety. In a few days put up a basic structure some twenty feet square. In four days, they had half the roof up, but cold and foul weather then hindered them. After they had a roof, they built the walls and packed them with mud. They figured out that houses would go up a lot faster if each man worked on his own. On January 9, "a reasonable fair day," they divided their town plan into individual lots.

On Thursday, January 11, the weather finally hit William Bradford. He was working on shore when all of a sudden he was shot through with pain. The pain had started in his ankles after wading ashore during the first discoveries. The most recent mid-winter dips had made him feel even worse. Now, suddenly, he hurt to his hipbones. He could not go on. He was ready to die. But God stepped in, and by evening, Bradford felt a little better.

Bradford, who as a boy had been too ill and weak for farm work, was now among the handful of people whose health had not faltered. Myles Standish would be about the only person to make it through the winter without falling ill, and he went far beyond the call of his duty as a military man to care for the ill and dying. The elder William Brewster also kept his health. Almost every day another person died, sometimes several persons. During the worst of the dying, only six or seven people were strong enough to prepare food, feed the ill, fetch wood, make fires, made beds, and change their "loathsome clothese." "In a word," Bradford wrote, "[they] did all the homely and necessary offices for them which dainty and queasy stomachs cannot endure to hear named."

They also had to bury the dead. If a few died each day for several days, a backlog of the deceased may well have lain among the living until the weather cleared or the handful of healthy men had the strength to move them. The chill would have slowed decomposition but not eliminated the odor that comes with death. When someone died aboard the ship, the healthy had to hoist the cold corpse up out of the gun deck (or out a gun port) and lower it down to the shallop or the longboat. They rowed the bodies in to shore, maybe passed them to someone on the famous rock, then carried them across the beach to somewhere where they could break the frozen ground. The sandy hill just above the beach was the easiest place, so that may have become the cemetery. English tradition would not have called for a hole six feet deep, and Calvinist beliefs would not have them mark a grave with a cross. Exhaustion and exigency probably conspired to let an even shallower grave suffice. To keep the Indians from detecting how quickly the English were dying off, they smoothed over the graves, left them level with the ground, and left them unmarked. The flesh of Christians rotted anonymously. It's likely that by spring, the survivors would forget where they had buried whom. Over a century later, in 1735, a spring flood would wash some of the remains down the hill and into the harbor. In 1855, workers found Pilgrim bones when they laid water lines along Carver Street.

The doctor trying to hold back the scythe of an unknown disease was deacon Samuel Fuller. Working without real medications or any awareness of the existence of germs, without much or any formal education in medicine, he treated people with herbs, hope, prayer, and beer. He may have used wormwood as a purgative, angelic root to prevent infection, yarrow for a headache, hyssop for lung problems, feverfew for fever. A wet green beet leaf across the forehead might also bring down a fever. Cranberries would have alleviated the scurvy, if that was indeed the problem, but nothing indicates that the settlers had discovered the bitter little berries yet. They probably hadn't, as the berries were out of season.

Under the medical philosophy of the day, Fuller tried to balance his patients' humors. In theory, every body was born with a personal combination of four humorous elements: warmth, cold, wetness, and dryness. A doctor could determine a person's natural balance by assessing his or her personality, be it choleric (hot headed, easily angered), sanguine (compassionate, of warm blood), phlegmatic (sluggish, unemotional), or melancholy, (sullenness and volatility). Anatomy came into it, with humors concentrated in certain areas of the body, some different for women than for men, different for the young than the old, with certain humors presiding in accordance with a person's personality.

When a person's humors got out of balance, the theory went, he or she fell ill. Diagnosis was a matter of determining the excess or insufficient humor. The cure was a matter of supporting the weak humor or counteracting the strong. A hot, dry fever indicated a need for something cool and wet — cucumbers, for example, or beer. In the case of a hot and sweaty fever, tapping off a little blood through a hole in the arm might remove some of the personal heat and humidity. The ideal state was the warm and moist body, the sanguine state. Peppercorns might bring heat to the patient who felt cold. A phlegmatic condition, brought on, perhaps, by sleeping while lying flat, allowing phlegm to build up in the chest, could be countered with a little tobacco smoke — hot and wet to cause the patient to cough up the cold, dry phlegm.

Fever and phlegm were Fuller's main problems, and his attempts to fend off death with beer, herbs and tobacco were barely breaking even. He'd lost six patients in December and would lose eight in January. One who would not see February was Degory Priest, who left a widow and two daughters back in Leyden, still hoping to join him in America someday. He also left his signature on the Association and Agreement.

Sometime before spring Fuller lost Edmund Margesson, of whom history remembers not a single detail except that he, too, signed the agreement. Fuller lost Alice Rigsdale, and he lost her husband, John. It may have still been January when he lost Thomas Rogers, who left an eighteen-year-old son alone in Plymouth, and a wife and three children impoverished in Leyden. In that month he may have lost Elias Story. The young man — too young to sign the Association and Agreement — a servant to Edward Winslow, and that's all that history remembers of him. It looked like Fuller was going to lose William Bradford, too, until God intervened.

Friday, January 12: a fair morning. John Goodman and Peter Brown went out with two others to gather thatch a mile and a half away. They took two Pilgrim dogs, one a mastiff, the other a spaniel. The blue sky grayed and soon shed a January rain. Goodman, Brown, and the dogs failed to return. The journalist wrote that Master Leavor (it may have been Governor Carver) and three or four others wandered through the rainy forest, hallooing and shouting, maybe praying, maybe cursing, surely keeping an eye out for savages. They went back and got more men to help. By night they had found no one. A painful night of rain and snow passed. The next day, twelve men went searching. All but certain that Indians were to blame, they carried loaded guns with lighted matches. Again, they found nothing.

Goodman and Brown hadn't been killed or captured. They were wandering through the forest, quite lost after chasing the stupid dogs, who had chased a deer around the lake. The only weapons they had were their sickles. Expecting to be working up a sweat and not away for long, they were "slenderly appareled" in the wrong clothes for a night spent soaking in the rain, shivering in the sleet, freezing in the snow, sleeping on the ground. When they heard lions roar nearby — at least they sounded like lions — they abandoned the dogs, scrambled up a tree, clung to branches, quivered in the breeze, tried to spend the night up there, but the cold forced them down. They spent the rest of the night at the base of the tree, listening for lions and holding the dogs to keep them from starting a fight that no man would want to break up. Maybe they held them for the warmth, too. They wandered all the next day before climbing a hill and spying the bay in the distance. When they got back, John Goodman had to have his shoes cut off his cold, swollen feet.

Sunday, January 14: Windy. Just at dawn, the people on the ship saw smoke on shore. The common house was burning. They couldn't tell whether the men who slept there had escaped or whether savages were attacking. There was gunpowder in the house, and Governor Carver and William Bradford were known to be bedridden with illness. The people on board wanted to go in to shore but had to wait for hours as the tide came in at its own sweet speed, unhurried by any human urgency. When the shallop finally arrived, they learned that a spark had set the thatch on fire, and it had burned in a flash. The roof structure was still sound, however, and everyone had gotten out in time. Several loaded muskets did not discharge.

It was God again, they were sure, testing them, but not too much.

Monday: "It rained much all day that they on shipboard could not go ashore," the journalist wrote, "nor they on shore do any labor but were all wet."

Tuesday, Wednesday, Thursday: "Very fair and sunny days, as if it had been in April, and our people, so many as were in health, wrought cheerfully."

Friday: Rain. By noon, they gave up trying to build a shed. In the evening, despite the dreary weather, John Goodman took his painfully frostbitten feet for a walk. He took the spaniel that had gotten him and Peter Brown into trouble the week before. Not far from home two big wolves showed up, hungry for a tender pet. The spaniel, continuing its reputation as an animal worse than useless, cowered between Goodman's legs, drawing the wolves closer. Goodman, unarmed, feet too sore to run, grabbed a stick and heaved it at the wolves. They scurried away but soon returned. Goodman took up a fence post, but the wolves seemed to recognize the lack of threat in a quivering spaniel and a man who could barely walk. "[The wolves] both sat on their tails," the journalist wrote, "grinning at him a good while, and went their way and left him."

Saturday: better weather. They get the shed put up. Now they can bring more provisions to shore. Life will be easier once they no longer have to row out to the ship and back. They are one shed closer to really living in New England rather than off the coast of it.

On Sunday they rested and held meeting on land. The journalist said nothing about what this first church in New England looked like, whether they crowded into the common house or just stood in a sunny spot or arranged logs as benches around a fire. We don't know whether they hastened through prayers and praise in a shivery matter of minutes or stayed all morning, broke for lunch, and came back for more, whether their public confessions included confessions of doubt about the purposes of the Lord who was reaping their loved ones at a terrifying rate. One thing's for sure: they didn't pass a collection plate.

For the next week, they worked in good weather, bringing food supplies to the shed, putting up houses. They built a house for the ill. New England's first hospital for Europeans was a cabin with a floor of dirt, a fireplace in the corner, a roof of marsh reeds, and a doctor working with roots, herbs, tea, beer, tobacco, and prayer to a demonstrably unmerciful God. Statistically, it wasn't a hospital as much as a hospice for the terminally ill.

Myles Standish's wife, Rose, may have been one of the first to die there. She expired on January 29.

Then more cold. Sleet. Two Indians were seen in the woods, but they ran away.

Chapter Eleven

February

As January turned to February, winter barely underway, wind and rain hit hard. The *Mayflower*, now unballasted by most passengers and supplies, swayed, bucked, tilted, heaved, yawed, pitched and rolled as if itching to break off from its anchor and sail away. On shore the wind blew so hard it ripped mortar from the walls of houses. Maybe it wasn't sub-zero cold, maybe not even sub-freezing cold, not every day, anyway, but for these weakened, over-worked people it was killer cold, the dank cold of sleet rather than the dry cold of snow, the wind-chilled cold of a winter beach, the kind of cold that lays siege to ill, malnourished bodies so that germs can finish them off. In the short, dark month of February, the cold killed seventeen of the eighty-seven people who had survived January. We don't know who or on what dates, but by winter's end, and as likely in February as any other month, the cold killed Sarah Eaton, the mother of a suckling child. The cold killed Moses Fletcher, a twice-married father of ten who died alone, his family having stayed in Holland, awaiting word that he'd built them a house. The cold killed Thomas Tinker. It killed his wife. It killed their son. It killed Richard Clarke, who shivered into death with no family to lay a warm hand on him. It killed Thomas English. It killed William Holbeck, not yet twenty-one, servant to the White family. It killed John Langmore, servant to the Martins until they died.

Friday, February 9: The cold continued. Work was almost impossible. On shore, they kept the fireplaces of the few houses good and hot. A spark ignited the roof of the sickhouse, but no one was hurt. Someone shot five geese. The journalist wrote that the goose meat was distributed among the sick. The same person found a dead deer. Indians had cut its antlers off, and a wolf was eating its flesh. The journalist did not note whether the settlers ate what the wolf had not.

A week later, in a cold, north wind under clear skies, a duck hunter hiding in reeds a mile and a half from Plymouth saw twelve Indians go by, headed for the plantation. He heard more. As soon as they'd passed, he rushed home and sounded the alarm. Myles Standish and Francis Cook, working in the woods, dropped their tools, rushed back, armed themselves and got the defense in order. After three months of wet and cold, the muskets weren't likely to fire. But the Indians never showed up. They were in the forest, stealing Standish's tools.

The next day, Standish called a meeting to establish some kind of military organization. They couldn't be running around like fools when the savages came at them for real. They didn't have firearms for all the men. Some of the men probably had military experience, but not all, and if any had fought, they'd never fought people hidden and scattered in the forest. They knew nothing of tactics. They had no chain of command, no contingency plans, nothing but dire necessity to bolster their courage when the enemy came howling at them from all sides. He was confirmed as captain and given the authority of command. Before they could decide much else, two Indians appeared at the top of the hill above the settlement, just a quarter-mile away. They signaled for the settlers to come up. The settlers took up arms and signaled for the Indians to come down.

This was a decisive juncture in history. On Standish's order, the settlers could have shot a preemptive volley at the savages, inspiring in them the fear of God, probably killing at least one, ideally scaring off the rest forever and ever. Or they could just walk up the hill into an ambush, the opening gambit in a full-scale attempt to wipe the invaders from the Indian continent.

Peace was preferable to war by far. As peace can begin only with gestures of trust, Standish and Stephen Hopkins decided to take a chance. Taking just one musket, they crossed the brook and approached the hill. In a gesture of peace, they laid the musket down. Both men, unarmed, proceeded to advance. They could hear a great many more Indians beyond the hill. It was a tense situation. The two men needed substantial courage to remain unarmed as they walked toward people who had been skulking around the plantation and shown no reluctance to shoot arrows at the settlers. Standish and Hopkins proved more courageous than the Indians, who took off before the Englishmen reached them.

From then on, the settlers kept their ordnance close at hand. Master Jones sent in a crew with a minion. They dragged it to the top of the hill and got to work on a wooden platform from which to operate it. They dragged another minion up there from the beach. Master Jones and the sailors also brought a fat goose and a fat crane, a mallard duck and a dried neat's tongue to share with the Planters. Defense is fine, but it works better on a full stomach.

Their defense couldn't be much more precarious. Midway through the winter, they had as few as thirty men and a handful of teenage boys to defend the settlement. They had no time to cut timber or put up a palisade in the frozen ground. If the savages attacked, a few musket and cannon shots would be followed by hand-to-hand combat in a rain of arrows. In about an hour, few dozen Indians could wipe out the settlement, leave nothing of the venture but bodies and ash.

On February 21, William White died, leaving his wife, Sussana, five-year-old Resolved, and little Peregrine, now two months old.

On the same day, William Mullins, New England's only shoe salesman, died, leaving his wife Alice, his teenage son Joseph, his seventeen-year-old daughter Priscilla, two children back in Europe, and twenty-one dozen pairs of shoes. His will offered to sell the whole lot of shoes to the community for 40 pounds, or, if that seemed too much, then he'd take, in absentia, anything reasonable.

On February 25, Mary Allerton, wife of Isaac, died, leaving children Bartholomew, Remember, and Mary. She also left somewhere in the dunes her stillborn babe.

The toll of February, to reach 17, would have to include a few others known to have died that winter. One might have been Ellen More, oldest child of the divorcing Mores back in England, now under the care of the Edward Winslow family. She was eight.

February may also have killed Edward and Anne (Cooper) Tilley, leaving their niece, Humility Cooper, 1, alone, her father already dead back in Europe, her impoverished mother back there, too. Humility may have been passed to Edward's brother, John, and his wife, Joan, if they were still alive. But if the cold hadn't already taken them, it soon would. In any event, by spring, Humility would have passed to the arms of her only living relative on that side of the ocean, her mother's second husband's brother's daughter, Elizabeth. She was 13.

The plague struck the sailors, too, taking a boatswain, a gunner, three quartermasters, the cook — in all, about half the crew of twenty-five or thirty. Master Jones began to worry that he wouldn't have enough men to sail back to England. Even if a skeleton crew survived, he'd have to wait until they were strong enough for the trip. As the passengers' beer ran out, the crew hoarded their own. Passengers were incensed that even the sick and dying were "forced to drink water." Witnessing the suffering of his own people, Master Jones began to empathize with his cargo of passengers. He told Governor Carver that even if his crew had to drink nothing but water all the way across the Atlantic, he would send beer to anyone who really needed it.

Meanwhile, Bradford reported that friction was rubbing among the crew raw.

> *They that before had been boon companions in drinking and jollity in the time of their health and welfare, began now to desert one another in this calamity, saying they would not hazard their lives for them, they should be infected by coming to help them in their cabins; and so, after they came to lie by it, would do little or nothing for them but, 'if they died, let them die.'*

Some of the crewmembers were pretty nasty to the passengers. In a beautifully Christian response, the passengers still on board turned the other cheek and returned ill will with good.

> *The passengers as were yet on board showed them what mercy they could, which made some of their hearts relent, as the boatswain (and some others) who was a proud young man and would often curse and scoff at the passengers. But when he grew weak, they had compassion on him and helped him; then he confessed he did not deserve it at their hands, he had abused them in word and deed. 'Oh!' (saith he) 'you, I now see, show your love like Christians indeed one to another, but we*

let one another lie and die like dogs.'

Another sailor, less enlightened, lay cursing his wife, saying had it not been for her, he never would have come on this "unlucky voyage." He cursed his sailor friends, accusing them of letting him die after all he had done for them. Another offered to leave his companion all he had if his friend would help him in his weakness. The friend got a little spice and a little meat and served him a meal or two. When the fellow failed to die, his companion went around saying he'd been duped into helping, that he would sooner choke this ailing friend than serve him any more meat. But the patient died before morning, and his friend reaped his coveted inheritance.

Chapter Twelve

March

March 3 dawned misty, with a warm, comfortable wind coming up from the south. At one o'clock, a loud thunderstorm came through. Until midnight it shed a rain that Bradford described as sad.

Four days later, the weather turned cold again as the wind swung around to come in off the ocean. Master Carver and five others went up to Billington's Sea to fish. We don't know whether they caught anything. They found evidence of many deer but saw none. Back at the plantation, the Planters sowed their first garden seeds, probably peas and greens.

People continued to die. At some point in March, the

William Mullin's widow, Alice, died. Her son, Joseph, died. Priscilla was left alone with a small fortune in shoes. Mullin's teenage servant, Robert Carter, also died. Ten others would die in March. One of them might have been James Chilton's widow, who died late in the winter, leaving her daughter, Mary, 13, an orphan in Plymouth. He also left six other children orphans back in Europe.

By winter's end, Isaac Allerton's servant, John Hooke, 13, died. Allerton's brother, John, died. He had intended to spend only that first winter in America, helping the family of his brother Isaac, then sail home to his wife.

John Turner died. One of his sons died. Then the other one died. John Crackstone died, leaving a teenage son of the same name. If the boy had a mother, she was back in Europe.

Edward Fuller and his wife died, leaving Samuel, 12, with his uncle, Dr. Samuel Fuller. And if it was in March that four-year-old Mary More, the youngest of the More children, died, she brought the month's toll to thirteen. Only her brother Richard survived. He was six. His parents back in England were almost free of the cause of their marital embarrassment.

On Friday, March 16, Standish again tried to get the men organized into some kind of militia. They had a lot to learn. The musket was an ineffective weapon that could be as deadly to its users as to their enemy. It was hard to get a matchlock to fire, yet it was easy to fire it by mistake. The source of its fire was a smoldering cord of hemp treated with saltpeter — the match. The match was clipped into a matchlock. Pulling the trigger activated the matchlock, tilting it and the match down to the small pan of gunpowder. If the match successfully lit the powder, it fed a flame into the breech. If the flame made it into the breech, it set off the charge that propelled the lead ball out the muzzle.

When expecting trouble, the musketeers would keep their muskets loaded. They wouldn't put powder into the pan until they were about ready to shoot. They carried their gunpowder in premeasured portions in wooden canisters strung on a bandolier around the neck. They might keep an extra lead ball in the mouth, where they could quickly get it when they needed it. They would keep both ends of the match lit, hoping that at least one end would still be glowing when the time came to shoot. Musketeers could not sneak through the woods with any degree of secrecy. The Pilgrim militia operated in a haze of hemp smoke. Sneaking up on a deer or an enemy was impossible.

Standish carried a flintlock musket called a snaphance. The flintlock mechanism fired more readily, maybe even in a light rain. Rather then use a lit match, it snapped a bit of flint against a bit of steel to drop a spark into the pan of powder. Once loaded, it could be fired in an instant, without the bother of messing with a match. The only drawback was that the flint didn't always make a spark. Odds of a misfire were about fifty-fifty, depending on the weapon and the weather.

Standish had to get his minuscule militia organized. The last thing they needed under the pressure of attack was some idiot touching his match to his pan prematurely, shooting off a six-tenths-inch ball of lead in the wrong direction. It was hard to get the ball to hit what it was supposed to hit, but when it hit, it killed. Striking flesh, it would flatten before plowing into the body. The exit wound would be the size of a fist. A person might survive a shot to a limb, but the limb would probably have to be amputated.

So the musketeers had to drill. Standish would bark them through the series of steps required to load and fire a matchlock musket:

Shoulder your piece! (to get everyone in step)

Unshoulder your piece! (to prepare to prepare it)

Blow out your pan! (to free it of stray grains that might ignite too soon)

Prime your pan! (by sprinkling a little powder into it)

Close your pan! (rotating a little lid over it)

Blow off your pan! (again, to free it of loose grains)

Open your charge! (i.e., open a wooden canister that

held powder)

Ram your powder! (into the muzzle)

Ram your ball! (into the muzzle)

Ram your wad! (into the muzzle)

Put it up! (i.e. put away the ramrod)

Take gun in hand! (while holding both ends of the match with the same hand that would pull the trigger)

Blow on your match! (one end, to get it glowing)

Fit your match! (into the matchlock)

Open your pan! (Careful now!)

Give fire! (Pull the trigger, dropping the matchlock and its glowing cord into the powder in the pan.)

Boom!

Unhook match! (to begin the process of reloading)

The maneuver required the musketeer to hold the match, which was a couple of feet long and lit at both ends. Two fingers held one end while two other fingers held the other end while the same hand supported the sixteen-pound musket and reached for the trigger. Fingers tended to get burned in the process. *Ow!* was not an option during training nor attack, nor was dropping one's musket to suck on a finger.

In the time it took to let off a shot and prepare for the next, an Indian with a bow could loose half a dozen arrows. The bow and arrow was not an inferior weapon. Not only did it shoot sooner and faster, but it always shot, even in rain, wind, and cold. In the hands of a skilled bowman, it was, up to a certain distance, as accurate as a musket. It didn't require one to carry balls, wads, powder for the shot, a finer powder for the pan, and a lit match. It didn't require a hunter to walk upwind, nor did its smell prohibit an ambush. The only advantages of the musket were its terrifying explosion, the distance it could throw its ball, and the deadly mess it made if it happened to hit its target.

So the settlers in Plimouth were outgunned by bows and arrows, not to mention outnumbered by a ratio they could hardly imagine. By spring, the little army could muster no more than twenty-five men and half a dozen boys over the age of twelve. They were surrounded by uncountable thousands of potential enemies who, sooner or later, would get used to the thunder of muskets. Myles Standish had his work cut out for him and very little time to turn these urban Christians into back-woods killers. So far, he'd lost half his troops without anyone getting hit by an arrow.

He'd hardly started the training process when, once again, as if on cue, the fledgling militia was interrupted by a savage, this time just one, buck naked but for fringed leather around his waist. He came striding resolutely, fearlessly, straight toward the settlement, revealing more male skin than the Pilgrim women had seen outside of their homes. Men rushed out to intercept him. In one of the most astounding moments in American history, this tall, black-haired savage from out of the woods made a gesture of friendship and said in an accent somewhere between Algonquin and cockney, "Welcome, Englishmen."

Documents surviving from the period do not record whether flabbergasted jaws dropped open, teeth fell to the ground, eyes popped from wide-stretched sockets, breath stopped short or words clotted in throats. The utterly impossible stood before them, a savage in command of the king's English and, as it turned out, a thirst for English beer.

In words thick with Algonquian accent, he told them his name was Samoset. They told him he had arrived too late. The beer was gone. But they were quick to serve him a snort of aqua vitae, some biscuits, butter, cheese, pudding, and a bit of mallard.

And there he sat. If God worked in mysterious ways, this was His most bizarre so far. Until that moment, though savages and Christians were often within shouting distance, they'd still been an ocean apart, unable to communicate except by shooting and howling at each other. Now, in an instant, they had a bridge of language. Samoset was less than fluent, but they could understand him.

That was the end of boot camp. They spent the day milking Samoset for all the information they could get. He told them they were standing in a place called Patuxet. The area had been populated by the Patuxet tribe, but they had died or fled. A mysterious disease had exterminated them some four years prior, after the first European ships arrived.

The specific disease has never been identified, but small pox, tuberculosis and Bubonic plague are suspected. Whatever it was, it was very lethal, wiping out all or almost all the Patuxet and cutting other tribes down to a fraction of their previous size. The scene in the Patuxet village must have been even more horrific than that of the *Mayflower's* gun deck during the worst of the winter. Most likely the Patuxet died in a short period. After several deaths, it would have been obvious that no one who caught the sickness would survive. Maybe parents saw their children die first. Maybe the children survived longer. How many of the dead got buried? How long until wild wolves moved in to take the unburied?

Years later, no one owned or claimed or even wanted the land around Plymouth. A miraculous combination of wind, waves, and winter had brought the Pilgrims to one of the few places on the planet that didn't belong to somebody.

Samoset himself was not of the nearby Pokanoket or Nauset tribes. He was a sagamore of the Pemaquid, a tribe up in Maine. Eight months earlier he and a friend had hitched a ride south on a ship commanded by Thomas Dermer, who had stopped by Monhegan Island, off the coast of Maine, to trade for furs. Samoset was spending the winter with the Pokanoket, the people of the sachem Massasoit. As for Dermer, he was dead, hunted down by Indians on the island of Martha's Vineyard, just south of Cape Cod.

The Patuxet and Nauset were in alliance with the Pokanoket, Massasoit's people. It was the Nauset who had been shooting arrows at the Pilgrims out on Cape Cod. They had good reason to shoot arrows at Europeans. It was just six years earlier that Master Thomas Hunt had kidnapped seven Nauset and twenty Patuxet and taken them to Europe. In another incident, as likely involving the French as the English, several Indians aboard a ship were mowed down with buckshot blasted at them by a murderer cannon. The Nauset weren't about to trust anybody else from a sailing ship. They were, in Bradford's words, "much incensed and provoked against the English," incensed and provoked enough to kill three of Sir Ferdinando Gorges' sailors the previous summer. When a French ship wrecked on Cape Cod, Indians pursued the survivors, killing all but three or four who were captured and sent around to the local sachems for torturous sport. Thomas Dermer rescued two of them. The Indians expected retribution. When they saw the

Mayflower, they figured retribution had arrived. Loosing a few arrows at its landing party seemed like a good idea.

When the arrows failed to scare off the invaders, the Nauset gathered their medicine men for an emergency curse. For three days, Bradford wrote, they met "in a horrid and devilish manner, to curse and execrate [the settlers] with their conjurations, which assembly and service they held in a dark and dismal swamp." Given the difficulties the settlers suffered, the curses and execrations seem to have been working well.

But Samoset said he could patch things up. He'd worked with a few Englishman, trading for pelts and showing them around. He knew that they weren't all bad. He named some names that the settlers recognized — Dermer, Hunt, Gorges, maybe Smith and Weymouth, too. Samoset knew Englishmen, and he knew the local people, including the sachem Massasoit, chief of a loose confederation of villages and tribes that would later coalesce and be known as the Wampanoag. The Wampanoag tribes inhabited what is today southeastern Massachusetts, Cape Cod, the islands of Nantucket and Martha's Vineyard, and the eastern part of Rhode Island. Indians and the Pilgrims identified the various Wampanoag tribes by the names of their villages. Massasoit, to them, was a Pokanoket, the name of a village not far inland from Plymouth. Among the Wampanoag were the Nauset, a tribe of a few hundred out on Cape Cod, the same who had been shooting arrows at the settlers when they first arrived. If there was anybody the settlers wanted to talk to, it was Massasoit.

Samoset spent the rest of the day with his new friends. They put a coat around his bare shoulders, fed him well and invited him out to the *Mayflower*. He was glad to go, but a wind came up and the tide was out. The shallop was stuck out at the ship. Samoset would have to spend the night in the settlement. Stephen Hopkins agreed to put the Indian up for the night.

They watched him as he slept.

The next morning, March 17, they sent Samoset on his way with a knife, a bracelet, and a ring. He promised to return within a day or two with some of Massasoit's people and some beaver pelts. Bradford told him that it would be nice if he and his friends brought back the tools that certain savages had swiped a few weeks ago when they attacked the woodcutters in the forest. Governor Carver let it be understood that if the tools weren't returned, the English would do something about it. Apparently he didn't mention the corn, kettle and trinkets his explorers had borrowed back in November.

Come Sunday, March 18, Samoset returned, bringing with him "five tall proper men" in deerskin leggings that reminded the Pilgrims of Irish trousers. Their leader wore wildcat skin on one arm. They all had long hair, some with feathers, one with a foxtail. They had the complexion of English gypsies. Some had their faces painted with a broad, black stripe from forehead to chin. At their hosts' request, they left their bows and arrows a quarter mile outside of town. They brought with them packs of powdered corn, a little bag of tobacco, and three or four furs. They also had the missing tools.

It wasn't the best of days for a visit. The Christians had their Sabbath worship to tend to, but courtesy and expedience took immediate priority. The English brought out food, and their guests helped themselves most liberally. Conversation was limited, of course, but the gestures were of friendship and respect. The guests sang and danced "like antics," an act that looked to the Europeans like so much after-dinner buffoonery but which may have expressed anything from thanks to digestive problems. Or maybe it was a pitch to buy pelts.

The Christians, however, were closed for business. Only savages would want to do business on a Sunday. Somehow Samoset got the message that on every seventh day, trading was a sin. He and the others agreed to come back in a few days. Despite the settlers' remonstrations, they insisted on leaving the skins until then. They trusted their English friends not to run off (and probably wouldn't have minded if they did), and besides, they didn't want to carry the skins back home. The settlers gave each of their guests a little gift and escorted them back to the stash of bows and arrows. A few other Indians shied away until their cohorts told them it was safe.

Samoset stayed behind in Plymouth, pleading or feigning illness; no one was sure. By Wednesday, he was still there, and the owners of the beaver pelts had not returned. The settlers loaded him down with gifts — a hat, shoes, socks, a shirt, a sash for the waist — and bade him fetch his friends back to settle the matter of the pelts.

March, meanwhile, was shifting from lion to lamb. The settlers planted their gardens. On March 20, they got back to the business of setting up a military order. And again, no sooner had they started than Indians arrived, this time just two, but armed and taunting from atop the hill. Captain Standish and another man took up muskets and went to investigate. Two other men backed them up from a polite but tactical distance. The Indians made a show of preparing arrows, but as Standish approached, they ran off.

It was on this day that the last of the settlers transferred from the *Mayflower* to Plymouth. Like children gradually pulling away from their mother's fold, they rowed out to the ship less and less. Their life was on shore. But the *May-*

flower was always out there, drifting around her anchor. If they wanted to go back to England, back to nice houses and good food, all they had to do was get on board. It was still their ship. All they had to do was say, "Home, Jones," and they'd be on their way.

Thursday, March 22, was a very fair warm day. At about noon, with everyone assembled on land for the first time, the people of Plymouth met for "public business." And once again they were interrupted. It was Samoset. He had with him a friend, Tisquantum, the only survivor of the Patuxet tribe. Tisquantum, it turned out, spoke excellent English, and he knew it for much the same reason that he had survived the plague. He wasn't in Patuxet when the disease struck. He was in shackles on the ship of a certain Master Hunt, bound for Spain.

Chapter Thirteen

Squanto

Despite their travails and tragedies, the Pilgrims had received a few miracles. When John Howland had washed overboard in the middle of the Atlantic, the halyard came into his hand. When the beam above the passenger had warped and cracked, all but dooming the ship, it held until someone remembered that they'd happened to have packed a big screw-type jack. When the winter sickness had hit almost everyone, not everyone had died. Then the land where they settled happened to be not only vacant of inhabitants but left with fields cleared and ready to plant. And then Samoset came along, not only speaking English but establishing peace with the neighbors.

An argumentative agnostic, on the other hand, might

point out such contramiracles as the late start out of England, the exceptionally harsh winter, and the deaths of two score Planters before they'd planted a single seed. But with the arrival of Samoset's friend, Tisquantum, even the most skeptical disbeliever would have to acknowledge the possibility of divine cooperation. Tisquantum was as close to miraculous as any American would ever be. He was a miracle so human and close to the earth that he had to have a nickname. They called him Squanto.

By the time the *Mayflower* arrived, Squanto had already been across the Atlantic at least twice, maybe as many as six times. The supposed first trip is the most dubious, supported by only scanty documentation. He may have been kidnapped in 1605 and taken to London to learn English and then to serve as a guide and translator for explorers of New England.

It is far more likely that his first transatlantic trip started in 1614, when two ships, one under John Smith, the other under a notorious scoundrel, Thomas Hunt. The ships arrived at Patuxet to trade for pelts and other goods. Once Smith had filled his ship, he sailed for England, leaving Hunt to dry a load of fish and buy as many beaver pelts as his ship could carry. He was then to sail for England.

But the Hunt had other plans. He lured seven Nausets and twenty Patuxets onto the ship, one of them Squanto.

There they found themselves slapped into shackles and soon headed east.

Hunt took his captives to Spain, where he sold them on the Malaga slave market. Some may have ended up in North Africa. A few, including Squanto, were rescued, possibly bought, by Dominican monks who may have wished to convert the savages to the Christian faith. A year or two later, Squanto made his way to London. There he lived in the Cornhill district with John Slanie, a wealthy merchant and treasurer of the Newfoundland Company. Slanie soon hired the young man to go to Newfoundland as interpreter and consultant. While in Newfoundland, Squanto met Master Thomas Dermer, an old friend of Master John Smith. Dermer got the idea that maybe Squanto could help mend relationships with the Nauset and Patuxet, who were still angry about the kidnappings by Thomas Hunt and Edward Harlow. Europeans landing anywhere around Cape Cod could expect a violent welcome. At Ferdinando Gorges's request, Dermer and Squanto sailed back to England to work on a plan. In 1619, Dermer and Squanto sailed for Cape Cod.

Squanto no doubt went straight to Patuxet, expecting tears of joy and warm greetings from his friends and family. But he found only a horror beyond comprehension. The village was empty of people, its grounds scattered with bones, its houses abandoned, everyone dead or gone. The disease had also cut neighboring tribes to a fraction of their size. Squanto had survived only because he'd had the good fortune to have been captured and sold into slavery. Only later would he find relatives living in Nemasket, fifteen miles to the west, and apparently that's where he went to live.

Dermer left Squanto with the Pokanoket and pressed on to the land of the Nauset, where he hoped to explain that Master Hunt was gone and wasn't coming back and that all Englishmen weren't as bad as he. Before he had a chance to explain, he was captured. They released him only after Squanto came to his rescue. Dermer, Squanto and Samoset sailed on to the island of Martha's Vineyard. There they met Epenow, the Wampanoag who had been captured by Edward Harlow and returned by Nicholas Hobson. Squanto and Epenow had both been the victims of kidnapping, but Epenow was less forgiving. He and his men attacked Dermer, mortally wounding him with arrows and killing several of his men. Epenow held Squanto and Samoset prisoner for having helped the English. He took them to the Pokanoket sachem, Massasoit, to dispose of at his pleasure.

Massasoit knew better than to waste compatriots who knew the English and their ways. The Pokanoket were in a touchy situation. The disease that had wiped out Squanto's tribe had decimated the Pokanoket and other nearby villages. Now at war with and partially under the control of their Narragansett neighbors to the west, the Pokanoket could not afford a mistake. Squanto persuaded Massasoit that the English, with their magnificent weapons, would be better as allies than as enemies. When the *Mayflower* came along a few months later, it was the Nausets of Cape Cod who attacked the landing party at First Encounter. Maybe Massasoit and Squanto later persuaded them not to continue the attacks, not even when the winter's sickness and malnourishment had left the invaders all but defenseless. (On the other hand, for all we know, the Nausets were waiting for nature to take its full toll before a welcoming committee went in to finish the job. Or maybe they were just waiting to see why the ship, unlike earlier traders, was staying so long.)

Whatever the unknown political machinations of the deep woods, Samoset knew the English well enough to dare a visit in the spring. He now returned with Squanto, three friends, some pelts to trade, a pile of dried herrings, and news: nearby was Ousamequin, the Pokanoket sachem commonly known as Massasoit. With him were his brother, Quadequina, and an entourage of sixty advisors and bodyguards. It wasn't clear what the English were supposed to do about Massasoit, but an hour later, he and his fellows appeared on the hill. Massasoit would not come down into town, and the English were unwilling to send the English sachem, Governor Carver, outside the fortification. Squanto went up the hill for a "powwaw" with Massasoit. Massasoit wanted to talk. The English decided to send Edward Winslow. He probably went with a certain reluctance and anxiety. His wife Elizabeth was sick with the symptoms that had proven so fatal to so many others. She might well succumb as so many others had. But Winslow had an important mission: to parlay money and peace. Elizabeth would have to do without him for a while.

Bradford described the visitors as tall and strong, some naked, some in furs, all with faces painted and free of whiskers. Massosoit's face was the deep red of mulberry. He was as young, strong, and able as the rest, dressed no differently except for a chain of white bone beads around his neck. Also at his neck he carried a pouch of tobacco and a knife.

Winslow approached the Indians with gifts: for Massasoit, a pair of knives and a copper chain with a jewel; for Quadequina, a knife and a jeweled earring; for those of lesser rank, a pot of aquavit, some biscuits, some butter. The gifts were accepted, and Winslow launched into a speech. He passed along King James' salute and desire that the Americans would accept the English with love and peace as friends and allies. The king wanted to trade, too, if the Pokanoket had anything of interest.

After Massasoit had eaten and drunk his fill, he passed the leftovers to his underlings. Though Squanto was apparently not doing too good a job of interpreting the speech, Massasoit grasped the idea of trade. He indicated an interest in Winslow's armor and sword, two things that Winslow was too smart to part with at any price.

So be it. Massasoit still wanted to talk. He left Winslow in the custody of Quadequina while he and twenty men laid down their bows and arrows and came down to the brook. Myles Standish, a "Master Williamson" (probably of the ship's crew, or it may have been the Planter Thomas Williams, who died before spring) and half a dozen musketeers went to the brook, exchanged gestures of respect, accepted a few Pokanoket to hold as hostage against Winslow's safe return, and negotiated a meeting to be held right then and there in a house under construction near the brook. The English laid down a green blanket for a rug and set out some cushions. The great white governor arrived with a fanfare of trumpet and drum and an escort of musketeers, probably the most highfalutin pomp Carver had ever experienced. He kissed the savage's hand and the savage kissed his. Massosoit's men were most impressed by the trumpet and tried to play it. The governor called for a drink. Massasoit "drank a great drought" of aquavitae and broke out in a sweat. Then they ate a little meat, passed the pipe, and talked peace.

They reached an agreement:

1. *That neither he nor any of his should injure or do hurt to any of our people.*

2. *And if any of his did hurt to any of ours, he should send the offender that we might punish him.*

3. *That if any of our tools were taken away when our people are at work, he should cause them to be restored, and if ours did any harm to any of his, we would do likewise to them.*

4. *If any did unjustly war against him, we would aid him; if any did war against us, he should aid us.*

5. *He should send his neighbor confederates, to certify them of this, that they might not wrong us, but might be likewise comprised in the conditions of peace.*

6. *That when their men came to us, they should leave their bows and arrows behind them, as we should do our pieces when we came to them.*

Lastly, that doing thus, King James would esteem of him as his friend and ally.

Bradford described Massasoit as of able body, grave

countenance, and spare speech. There was nothing "wild" about this Indian, nothing savage in his ways. During the negotiations, he trembled with fear but held his ground — a clear sign of true courage.

Discussions done, they all returned to the brook — all but the hostages, who were held pending Winslow's safe return. Carver and Massasoit embraced, and the Indians went back up the hill. It wasn't Winslow who returned, however. It was Quadequina and a few others, apparently seeking some of the entertainment they'd missed. The English indulged them for a while, then sent them off to get Winslow, who soon arrived, but not in time to see his wife alive. The cold had taken her on March 24. They'd been married not quite three years.

Several Pokanoket seemed to think they were going to hang around, but Bradford sent them on their way. Only Samoset and Squanto remained, spending the night. Massasoit and his people, including wives and children, camped half a mile away. They said they'd be planting corn on their side of the brook and would spend the summer tending it. The settlers kept good watch all night, but the woods remained silent.

The next morning, several Pokanoket showed up, apparently hoping for some of that good English food. They also had a message. Massasoit wanted his new friends to come for a visit. Myles Standish and Isaac Allerton went — the journalist doesn't tell us where — and were treated to ground-nuts (a small tuber) and some tobacco. They came back safely. It was one of several good signs that the peace agreement was working. Chance encounters in the forest had not turned threatening. Indians came to visit the village. Governor Carver had them bring the king's kettle which the English filled with peas they'd brought from England.

But the agreement carried a downside, the part about mutual military assistance. The Pokanoket were at war with the Narragansetts. Massasoit was counting on the support of the ultimate weapon — the muskets that made such terrifying noise and struck from such a distance. The journalist mentioned this but made no note of fear, concern, or controversy about getting involved in a local war. The conflict between the two tribes could easily lead the settlers into a disastrous crisis, a war to prevent a war. Until such a crisis came to pass, the Pokanoket's conflict with the Narragansetts was ensuring their alliance with the settlers.

At some point in this cultural tension and political complication, John Billington got into some kind of argument with Myles Standish. We know little of the incident except that Billington was accused of using "opprobrious speeches" in "contempt of the Captain's lawful command."

Apparently the people met and decided to restore order and respect by tying Billington's neck to his heels. Billington groveled, "humbling himself and craving pardon," until folks took pity and forgave him for this first offense.

Friday, March 30: a fair day. Samoset and Squanto were still around, but there were no other Indian visitors. Everybody got back to work building houses. They also, finally, got some military orders established and laid down a few laws that applied to their new little civilization. At about noon, Squanto went off to fish for eels, came back that night with all he could lift in one hand. They were nice eels, fat and sweet. There was a trick to it, Squanto explained. You wade through the mud in bare feet. When you step on an eel, it squirts up out of the mud. Then you just grab it.

On this day they chose John Carver to be their governor for a year. He'd been governor of the ship as it crossed over. Bradford called him "a man well approved." Carver had shown wisdom, patience, and restraint in their relationship with the savages, and he had seen everyone through the deadly sickness. Those who had not died were growing stronger as the days grew warmer. Squanto, the miracle from out of the woods, had come to save them, and the first seeds were already in the ground. Houses had been built. If anyone objected to a Carver administration, no one recorded the controversy.

March became April. No one had died for several days. They had enough housing for everyone to sleep indoors. The ship's crew had recovered from their illness. The weather was warmer. It was time for the *Mayflower* to return to England. Master Jones had never intended to spend the winter. As an experienced ship master and part owner of his vessel, he had probably been sure to include demurrage in his contract so that he could be paid for the time he had to spend in port. The five-month delay had not been his fault. The ship had left England too late in the year, and then the passengers were slow in moving their goods to shore, and then the crew took sick. Those crewmembers who did not die were too weak to sail a ship across the ocean under a winter wind.

If he felt he deserved demurrage, he would have to wring it from the Adventurers back in London. He certainly wasn't going to get it out of the Planters. Their first payment to the Adventurers still stood unfelled in the forest, scampering in the underbrush, and swimming in the sea. If the Planters had arrived in summer, as originally planned, they might have had time not only to settle but to produce a little something to send back to England. Winter, however, allowed no labor beyond the minimum needed for hand-to-mouth survival. The summer of 1621 might have given the Planters time to make the first installment on their debt, but the ship could not wait. Food supplies for the crew were low. The beer was gone. The crew would have to drink water for the whole trip. Jones had the option of waiting until later in the year, giving the Planters time to prepare a cargo, but Jones had no reason for such optimism and no obligation to wait. April's showers would see the *Mayflower* headed for home.

The lack of cargo meant a lack of ballast. The *Mayflower* had to carry something of weight in its hold, so it loaded up with something heavy, probably cobble stones from the beach. England was not known to suffer a shortage of rock, so the loading must have included a certain sensation of guilt on the Planters' part.

Conscientious leader that he was, John Carver must have sent a letter back with the *Mayflower* to explain the load of rocks and lack of made-in-America goods. Though no such letter exists today, we can guess that if it ever existed, it bore the most heartbreaking excuse ever offered for not completing an assignment. Forty-five dead out of a hundred and two, two births balanced by two stillbirths, the survivors living hand to mouth, only a few shelters up, snow barely off the ground, not one fur-bearing animal trapped, and precisely one cod successfully brought to shore. He may have mentioned that, with the *Speedwell* still back in England, they had no fishing ship and thus couldn't be expected to do much serious fishing. He may also have mentioned the paucity of Adventurer support and the delays brought on by the financial and contractual bickering back in England.

Besides offering excuses, Carver must have asked for supplies. At the very least the settlers needed harpoons, small fish hooks, basic foods, gun powder, seed, and either malt or beer. They also needed new people. They had half the hands they'd left with yet had barely begun construction and planting. They'd be lucky to receive equipment or equipment and supplies before the next winter. Maybe, just maybe, if the winds were just right and the *Mayflower* reached England in a month and was immediately restocked, turned around, and sent back on more good winds, it might arrive by the middle of July, maybe early August.

Given their history since they first left Scrooby for Leyden in 1608, the Separatists had no reason to expect any such best-case scenario. If things went as they had so far, they'd never hear from England again. Instead of a *Mayflower* full of food, tools and people, they'd get a pirate ship full of cannons. But miracles, they knew, happened. God would take care of them. On April 5, the *Mayflower* weighed anchor, hoisted sail, and eased toward the eastern horizon, but it carried no Planters. Everyone stayed. If there was a moment when they became Americans, this was it.

Chapter Fourteen

Spring

From mid-April to mid-June they planted Indian corn. April might have been a little early, but it depended on the weather. Modern hybrid corn sprouts only when the ground reaches a consistent fifty to fifty-five degrees, which may not happen in New England until mid-May. Indian corn may have sprouted at cooler temperatures. In either case, seed planted too soon will rot. But Squanto knew the trick to the timing of it. He didn't look at (or have) a calendar. He looked at the buds of the white oak. When they grew to the size of mouse ears, it was time to plant corn.

But of course it wasn't that easy. Corn isn't a weed. It's a human invention, a product of old-fashioned genetic engineering, a crop that needs human attention from planting to harvest. It wasn't the natives of New England who invented it. Most likely it was an import from Mexico, where natives selectively planted tiny kernels from teosinte grass. Over the course of centuries, they developed a cob with seven rows of kernels. By about 6,000 BC, they had a highly productive and useful plant they called maize. Little by little, maize technology worked its way to the north and east. It arrived in New England about a thousand years before the English. The Pokanoket knew it well. They knew it grew better in the ashes of a field that had been burned. They knew it got along with beans, which naturally grew up around the corn stalk. They didn't know that the beans fertilized the corn by adding nitrogen to the soil. They figured out that squash liked to wander among corn stalks, picking up light where it could. The squash leaves shaded the ground, discouraging weeds from growing and the ground from drying out under direct sunlight. Corn, beans, squash, and Pokanoket all got along just fine.

But a kernel just stuck in the ground did not become corn. Raising corn was a lot like raising children. It needed constant attention. For fields in bad soil, Squanto explained, the planting of corn started with the catching of lots of fish. This first step must have dismayed the Planters. As fishermen, they were failures who had neither hooks nor a boat that could go far from shore. Squanto and his compatriots had hooks, but cod, they said, wasn't the way to go, not if you just wanted fertilizer. They trapped their fertilizer — alewives — in weirs in streams. The second step to planting corn, then, after checking the white oak buds, was to cut sticks of a certain length. These they stuck in the mud of streams to build mazes that an alewife could swim into but not out of.

The fish came in mid-April, just in time for the corn, rushing in great numbers up the very brook that ran through Plymouth. So many fish came so quickly and with such urgency that rock dams could not restrain them. They leaped over, sometimes even tumbling onto dry land. Catching a fish was a lot like catching a ball or manna from heaven. Like so many apostles at Galilee, the Planters waded into the brook to snatch as many fish as they could. Perhaps the gush of food coming up the brook, brought to mind a line from Psalm 36: *They shall be abundantly satisfied with the fatness of thy house; and thou shalt make them drink of the river of thy pleasures.* The alewives, it turned out, weren't just good for fertilizer. Cousins to the herring and shad, they were good to eat, too, so fatty they could be fried without grease. They could be preserved by smoking, too. The fishermen saw the future, and it was sweet — ships stuffed with smoked and salted alewives sailing back to Europe to pay off debts and puff up profits.

As for the corn, Squanto showed them how to arrange the fish to best replenish depleted soil. They were to raise mounds a few feet apart. In each mound they were to bury three alewives, their heads pointed toward the center. In the center, they were to plant a few kernels and some beans. As the corn grew, they were to pull up soil around the bottom of the stalk. They could use the same mound a year later, probably without adding fish.

Next, the wolf problem. The tempting aroma of rotting fish would draw wolves from the woods. If the corn patch weren't guarded day and night, the wolves would dig it up, dispersing the corn, ruining the harvest before it sprouted. The Planters would have to guard it for two weeks — long enough for the alewives to rot. They kept an eye out for wolves, but then it was their mastiff and spaniel who got into the fish. The solution: hobble the dogs. Then it was just a matter of weeding the patch for three months, keeping away the woodchucks, rabbits, crows, deer, and raccoons, and praying for rain.

Squanto showed them the herbs of the woods, taught them which were sweet, which bitter, which medicinal, which good for what. He pulled succulent roots from the ground. He showed them where the berries grew best, where best to find nuts. As the seasons came around, he took them to raspberries, blackberries, gooseberries, strawberries. They found five kinds of grape, one smacking of muscatel. He told them when the sweet, fat eels swam upstream to spawn, when they came back down, bitter and thin, to the sea. He took them to a river northeast of Plymouth where in May the smelt ran so thick they could be scooped up with bowls or flipped to the bank with a piece of bark. He took them halfway across the harbor to a place where they could find sea bass and bluefish five feet long. He took them to streams where from May through August they could net these fish by the hundreds. He took them twenty miles to the south side of Cape Cod, where they could find oysters as broad as bushel baskets. He showed them how to snare deer, dig clams, stomp eels from the mud, and bake corn bread. He taught them a new word: succotash.

It was during April's corn-planting that Governor John Carver suffered a problem still endemic each spring among gardeners in New England. As the earth turns warm and exudes a certain aroma of humus, gardeners drop to their knees and sink their fingers into the soil. They hack at it with hoes and turn it over. They poke seeds into the ground, pull soil over them, give the soil a little pat. If they see any connection between the miracles of winter becoming spring and seeds becoming life, if they have any idea of all that can go wrong before the harvest, they plant each seed with a prayer and fertilize it with thoughts to the effect of *please*. As if the length of rows might please God and buffer them from vermin, they open plots and fields limited only by darkness, calluses, back pain, and their endurance of gnats. In short, they work too hard.

Governor Carver was out there, too, planting as if his life depended on it, until the sun pushed him staggering from the field. He dragged his aching head to the coolness of his house, took a drink of water, and lay down on his bed, perhaps groaning the words of Psalm 22: *I am poured out like water, and all my bones are out of joint: my heart is like wax; it is melted in the midst of my bowels.* In a matter of hours, his senses failed him. His people applied prayer, but in a matter of days, he lay dead.

His death was much lamented and caused much heaviness among his people. Since Leyden his patience and wisdom had held them together through the wrenching stress of death after death, hunger upon cold, fear worsened by exhaustion and weakness. He stilled arguments between Saints and Strangers, between passengers and crew, between loyalists and those who would go their own way. He had made decisions untainted by self-interest. He had nurtured the sick during the great dying. He had helped bury the dead. In the spring, he had his hands in the soil. Unlike governors back in England, he had stooped to serve the people he led. He'd been healthy as the winter took life after life, then died as spring brought life back to the land. They buried him in warm earth and saluted him with volleys shot by all men who had arms.

Bradford described Governor Carver's wife, Katherine, as "a weak woman" who could not survive the loss of her husband. Within a few weeks, she followed her beloved to wherever it is the good Pilgrims go.

The trials of the winter had left William Bradford weak, too, but soon after Carver's death, he was elected governor. His weakness was a bad sign, and life was by no means a sure thing, so they did not delay in electing an assistant governor. Isaac Allerton was the man.

As the warmer weather thawed the ground, they were able to build better houses. Now they could dig clay, mix it with water, in effect pulling up the earth to make shelter of it. They didn't have enough carpenters to build everyone's houses. Rather, their few experienced carpenters advised everyone else how to do it themselves. Printers, servants, weavers, and wool combers became house builders. The architecture was simple and expedient. They started with four corner posts set into the ground, then connected them with horizontal beams. Across the beams they set rafters. Before they set the vertical studs, they put up the roof. The roofs were steep, high, layered with overlapping bundles of marsh reeds or cattails. Later, more ambitious builders would cut cedar shingles. But people not inclined to cut shingles to just the right shape (a process that might well begin by roaming the woods in search of a cedar) found reeds easier to deal with. Also, each shingle needed two nails that would have to be brought in from England. Reed roofs needed no nails, leaked less, and when they did leak, were easily plugged with a new bundle of reeds. With the occasional plug and replacement, a reed roof could last more than fifty years.

After they had a roof up, they could build the walls — first the vertical studs, then between them a lattice of sticks, called wattles. The wattles they packed with clay mud, called daub, which they mixed by tromping in it. The roof had to go up first so that rain couldn't wash the wet daub away. Wattle and daub construction had been used in England since the Middle Ages and would be used in America for centuries to come. The Plymouth settlers had no lime to mix into a waterproof plaster, so they used clapboard to keep the outside walls from eroding. They cut the clapboard by slicing it from logs. The slicing, or riving, tool was a frow, a blade at a right angle to two handles. They banged on the frow with a beetle, then smoothed the slice of wood with a spokeshave.

When they got around to building chimneys, they used

the same wattle-and-daub structure. Until then, they just let fireplace smoke rise up and waft through the thatch roof. The women cooked on hearths ten feet wide or more. The hearth dominated its house. People ate beside it and slept just a few feet away in a bedroom demarcated by nothing more than a curtain around a bed. It wasn't until the next summer, at the earliest, that some of the houses may have added a loft for storage and perhaps a place for a servant to sleep.

Windows in that first year were open holes in the wall with shutters to cover them. Late in the year, when Edward Winslow sent a letter back to England advising future immigrants what to bring, he suggested paper and linseed oil. Rubbed with the oil, the paper would become translucent, becoming a window that would let in light but not draft.

On May 12, Plymouth held its first marriage. Susanna White, widow of William (and mother of Resolved and the infant Peregrine), married Edward Winslow, widower of Elizabeth. Significantly, an elected magistrate, not a church official, performed the wedding. Because the Bible says nothing about ministers performing weddings, the Separatists believed the ceremony to be a civil, not religious, matter. Bradford cited Dutch law as the model he was following. (In England, the wedding was a religious event.) He did not say who pronounced Winslow and White man and wife. As elected governor, he himself probably officiated.

On June 18, something exploded between two young men, Edward Doty and Edward Leister, both servants of Stephen Hopkins. History leaves no record of the cause of the argument, but to them, at the time, death was the only reasonable resolution. They fought a duel, stabbing at each other with swords and daggers. One got wounded in the hand, the other in the thigh. Both were arrested and punished by being tied into agonizing positions, probably the ankles back to the buttocks, the head between the knees, the arms behind the back. The position caused so much suffering that Governor Bradford felt pity, probably saw a lesson quickly learned, and had them released "upon promise of better carriage."

Chapter Fifteen

Massasoit

Between the lines of *Mourt's Relation* one can detect hints of annoyance with the visits of Pokanokets. The settlers were apparently quite glad to receive Massasoit, Samoset, Squanto, and Quadequina. Continued peace, dialogue, and trade were important, but the visits of the hoi polloi were wearing thin. Each visit called for gestures of generosity to guests who were especially eager for foreign food. Generosity with good neighbors was fine, but enough was enough.

> *But whereas [Massasoit's] people came very often, and very many together unto us, bringing for the most part their wives and children with them,*

> *they were welcome; yet we being but [newcomers]*
> *at Patuxet, alias New Plymouth, and not know-*
> *ing how our corn would prosper, we could not lon-*
> *ger give them such entertainment as we had done,*
> *and we desired still to do. . .*

In other words, they wanted to make their neighbors feel welcome, but not too many of them. They were living off the dwindling supplies they'd brought from England, had already run out of beer, and were by no means sure they would reap, come autumn, what they had sowed. The solution: a mission to Massasoit to seek understandings on various issues.

The importance of the mission and its message required ambassadors who were comfortable and capable in conversation with Indians. Stephen Hopkins, who had put up Samoset when he spent the night, was one of them. Edward Winslow, who was taking an interest in, maybe even an appreciation of, the natives and their culture, was the other.

The mission was also one of reconnaissance. Bradford wanted to know where the tribe lived and how strong it was. He also wanted a better idea of the lay of the land. He also wanted it strongly implied that if Pokanoket could enter Plymouth safely, the settlers wanted to feel safe going into Pokanoket.

With Squanto's help, the emissaries were to explain, as delicately as possible, that Massasoit and his messengers were welcome in Plymouth, especially if they had furs to trade, but there just wasn't enough food and time for every visitor, not to mention wives, and brood, who wanted an easy meal. Hopkins and Winslow were also to reiterate the importance of peace and friendship. They took a gift, a horseman's coat, trimmed with lace, to indicate their most sincere desire to keep all doors open.

They had a plan for limiting visitors or at least preventing disinformation coming from messengers who said they spoke for Massasoit. To avoid the both needless entertainment of a false messenger and the denial of a true messenger, the settler's ambassadors would leave a copper chain with Massasoit. Any messenger carrying the chain was to be accepted as a rightful representative.

This would also be a good time to bring up the corn that the explorers had found in their first days on Cape Cod. They really did want to pay for it with some corn meal or some other staple they still had in stock. They would also consider accepting corn seed in exchange for seeds from England.

On the morning of July 2, Hopkins, Winslow, and Squanto headed for Nemasket, "a town under Massasoit, and conceived by us to be very near because the inhabitants flocked so thick upon every occasion amongst us." But they had conceived wrong. It was fifteen miles to Nemasket, near modern-day Middleboro, Mass. Along the way they met a dozen of the people who had been pestering them. They came along for the walk to Nemasket. They arrived midafternoon and were received with corn bread, shad roe, boiled acorns and joy. "After this, they desired one of our men to shoot a crow, complaining what damage they sustained in their corn by them." A few shots scared fourscore off and killed a few.

Though it was already late, Squanto wanted to press on another eight miles to a place that had better food. The English, being in somewhat of a rush to finish their expedition, agreed to continue. By sundown they came upon men fishing for bass at a weir on a river. In a gesture worthy of the Christian Savior, the savages shared their fish with the travelers. The travelers, confident that they would be well received in the future, shared the victuals they had brought. The fishermen said they didn't live there. They were just camping in a nearby field while they fished. This was still a place of plague where no one settled. Thousands of people used to live along the river, they were told, but now the population was of human remains lying where they had fallen or carrion animals had dragged them. "They not being able to bury one another," Bradford wrote, "their skulls and bones were found in many places lying still above the ground where their houses and dwellings had been, a very sad spectacle to behold."

Surely the Englishmen must have found the scene not much different from what might have happened to their own people that first winter had the weather been just a little colder, the germs a little stronger, the people a little less resistant and determined to survive. English germs had almost done to the English what they had done to the Patuxet.

Right across the bay, the Narragansett still lived, strong and untouched by the plague, a continuing threat to the weakened Pokanoket and their allies.

Winslow and Hopkins followed the ghoulish scene six miles up a river to a ford. The Indians suggested that the gentlemen might like to take their breeches off for the crossing. The journalist declines to report whether modesty ruled over discomfort. The subject changes as two old men, possibly the last of the Patuxets besides Squanto, appeared on the other side of the river. The old men waited until everyone was in the river, then charged, bows loaded, threatening to shoot if the men in the river didn't turn around and go back where they came from. Someone did some fast talking, convincing the old men that they weren't enemies. The bows lowered. The travelers crossed. Greetings were exchanged, perhaps apologies, too. The old men shared "such food as they had," and the English "bestowed a small bracelet of beads on them." One of the men — probably Winslow — kept a journal of this journey and noted that they were now sure the tide ebbed as well as flowed. It is not known whether he was referring to the tide of the river or the give-and-take of the what-goes-around-comes-around tide of life.

Refreshed, they pushed on. They passed many places that had once been inhabited, with open fields now in weeds taller than a man. They went through forests of oak, walnut, fir, beech, and "exceedingly great" chestnut trees, monumental columns maybe eight or ten feet in diameter and a hundred feet tall. Some places were rocky above ground and in the soil. The day was hot but springs and brooks were plenty. The Indians, however, would not drink from brooks or rivers, only from springs. At brooks, they offered to carry the English or their clothes or muskets. The kindness was noted in the journal.

They spotted a man. The Indians feared he might be a Narragansett. The settlers prepared their muskets, told their friends that even if twenty Narragansett came at them, they would fight them off. But the man turned out to be a friend of the Indians. He and several women were just fetching water, which they shared with the English. Farther on, they met another man with two women, returning from the beach with roasted crab, fish, and dried shellfish. Again the Indians shared their food, and the English repaid the kindness with beaded bracelets for each of the women.

They came to a village where they were treated to oysters and fish. From there they hiked on to Pokanoket, near modern Bristol, Rhode Island, only to receive bad news: Massasoit was not home.

But he could be fetched. When they heard he was on his way, Squanto suggested a two-gun salute. As soon as the men picked up their muskets the women and children panicked and ran off. They could not be persuaded to return until the men had laid down their arms and Squanto had explained the salute. Massasoit arrived to a double boom worthy of the gods. He then invited the guests into his house. There they set the horseman's coat upon his shoulders and draped the copper chain around his neck. "He was not a little proud to behold himself," the journalist wrote, "and his men also to see their king so bravely attired."

And then down to business: more peace and fewer pests. Massasoit agreed. He also would send someone to Paomet for corn seed.

That settled, Massasoit gathered his men around him and gave a great speech. As far as the English could tell, he was reiterating his leadership, impressing one and all with his intentions of peace, directing everyone to bring furs to the Pilgrims in his name. His men interrupted with applause as he named village after village. It took a long time.

They then settled down for a smoke and a chat about England and the majesty of the great King James. Massasoit marveled that such a great king could live without a wife. Impressed, the Indian king declared that James was his man and that the French were not welcome in his territory.

Oddly enough, Massasoit offered no food, apparently because he had just arrived home. But when it was obvious that the English were exhausted from their trip, Massasoit and his wife made room for them on their bed. The bed consisted of planks a foot off the ground and covered with a mat. Two other chiefs snuggled in as well, "pressed by and upon us." Lice and fleas pressed in, too. In barbarous tones, the Indians sang themselves to sleep. Winslow and Hopkins did not sleep well. In a moment of ingenuous poesy, the journalist wrote "we were worse weary of our lodging than of our journey."

After three nights of these strange bedfellows and an interminable meal of boiled fish, Winslow and Hopkins thought that they'd better head for home before their strength was sapped from lack of sleep. They bought a partridge to eat along the way, and before sunrise on a Friday, eager to get home for the Sabbath, they took their leave. Massasoit, "grieved and ashamed" of the limits of his entertainment, implored them to stay. Lightheaded with sleeplessness, the Pilgrims begged off. They had to go. Squanto stayed behind, retained by Massasoit to tour the local villages to spread the word that the skins of fur-bearing animals should be directed to Plymouth for trade. Six Indians escorted the men.

The partridge wasn't enough to get them home. They stopped at the village where they'd been treated so well before. There they partook of some fish, bought a handful of corn meal and a string of dried shellfish, big as oysters. The shellfish they gave to their escorts, and the corn meal they shared as they hiked along. They also paused to pass around a pipe of tobacco. Somewhere along the way, one of their Indian escorts got mad about something and ran off. The others led the English five miles out of their way to a house where they hoped to find some food, but no one was home. They hiked five miles back to the trail, by nightfall arriving at the weir in the river. Again, no one was there, no food available. But an Indian shot a shad in the river and a squirrel. They also caught some fish. They sent two Indians ahead to Plymouth to request that a decent meal be prepared. That night, at two o'clock in the morning, a violent thunderstorm blew in, dumping so much rain that it put their campfire out. Maybe they hunkered wet misery, but more likely they thought of their crops. *He shall come down like rain upon the mown grass: as showers [that] water the earth.* They hiked through the rain all the next day. They stopped at Nemasket, came in out of the rain, ate what the savages offered. Hunched within the low, smoky dome of animal skins, no doubt shoulder-to-shoulder with wide-eyed Nemaskets crowded around a small cookfire, they passed around gifts to anyone who showed kindness. But they gave nothing to one man — the one who had abandoned them the day before. The journalist is unclear as to the exact problem, but the English did not hesitate to chastise him for certain "discourtesies." A theft of tobacco may have been involved. When the man offered them a smoke, they declined, explaining that their God would destroy them if they accepted stolen goods. Other people in the little house seemed to appreciate this. Apparently even savages appreciated the snubbing of a bum.

Chapter Sixteen

The Pokanoket

The ancestors of the Pokanoket tribe inhabited the area west and south of Cape Cod 10,000 or 12,000 years before the *Mayflower* arrived. Until then, the area was under a glacier. As the glacier melted and receded to the north, it left behind a rocky, boggy region not unlike that of modern New England. Fifteen hundred years before the *Mayflower*, the local people were farming, forming pottery, sculpting soapstone, and hunting with the bow and arrow. To hunt fish, they used the same technology the Europeans were using then and still use: the harpoon, the net, the hook, the line, and the sinker. They planted much as the Europeans did, setting the seeds, keeping them watered, and scaring off the crows. They hunted and fished for their protein.

Feeding themselves was rarely a problem. With just a few hours of work each day, they lived as well as they wanted.

Pokanoket knowledge was different from European knowledge. They did not have or need such inventions as the wheel, the sail, the rudder, the arch, or the firearm. Their society was functioning quite well without such technology. While Europeans needed these "advanced technologies" to provide their cities with food and water, the quality of life in those cities wasn't necessarily better than it was in Pokanoket and other villages of the area. European cities were stinking places with garbage and sewage in the streets, where disease was widespread and often endemic, rats were rampant, public water was dangerous to drink, foods were often rotten, almost everyone drank an unhealthy amount of alcohol, and wars were fought with a technology-sharpened savagery beyond the imagination of the "savages" of North America.

Indians had long suffered many of the same illnesses that Europeans knew, among them arthritis, rheumatism, colds, and fevers, and their wounds got infected just as European wounds did. But until the Europeans arrived, the natives of North America had never experienced the diseases that are common among dense populations. Measles, smallpox, typhus, tuberculosis, bubonic plague, and diphtheria were unknown until their germs arrived by ship and quickly spread across the continent. The Indians' freedom from these diseases was, of course, their downfall. They had no immunity and little resistance, so diseases that were serious in Europe were deadly in America.

It is questionable whether the technologies that made European cities possible would have improved Indian society. The first European explorers who met Indians in New England found them to be beautiful, healthy, and, until they learned European ways, friendly and generous. Champlain called them handsome. Verrazano said, "They exceed us in size," and exhumed skeletons have indicated some may have grown well over six feet tall, taller than most Europeans. Their teeth were described as white strong, and regular, even among the elderly. Dutch, English, and French explorers considered the women attractive. Verrazano called them "very graceful and well formed: of a sweet and pleasant countenance." Champlain found them neat in manners and dress. Adriaen Van der Donck found them physically well favored and rarely ugly. Gabriel Archer noted the women's strength. Various Europeans noted that they saw no children with the deformities brought on by disease or malnutrition.

While the Europeans saw history as a linear process moving from simplicity and primitiveness to technological sophistication and, soon, the end of the world, the natives of North America generally saw life as a cyclical process. It wasn't moving forward in the sense of bigger accomplishments, distance from nature, and some sort of climactic end. It was moving in circles, from season to season, from life to death to life. While Christians were preparing for the world to end, Indians were preparing for it not to. While Europeans were consuming as much as they could and now needed a whole new continent to consume — its plants, minerals, and animals — the natives of North America had devised a sustainable system that didn't demand the conquering of new lands and peoples.

Pokanoket expertise was oriented around the simple use of things they found in nature, with only the most direct conversion into manufactured products. They could fashion fibers into string, reeds into mats, shells into hoes, stones into hammers, claws into arrowheads, trees into boats, bark into houses, saplings into traps, sticks into weirs, fish into fertilizer, mussels into money. They could mash copper ore into metal, though they had no idea how to smelt it. They could make fire, probably with a bow whose twine spun a stick that used friction to create an ember. That and the bow and arrow were their most sophisticated technology. They went one, big, conceptual step beyond the simple refashioning of one material into something similar but useful.

Indians also had their own medical technology. They

knew the curative powers of dozens of plants. They could treat colds with dogwood bark and fevers with cedar leaves, settle a cough with the inner bark of the wild black cherry, set bones with a cast of bark and resin, counteract frostbite with fir balsam, stop bleeding with spider web, stop diarrhea with oak bark, ease inflammation with wood ash, purge the bowels with skunk oil, cure hemorrhoids with bear grease, cleanse the kidneys with sarsaparilla, protect skin with eagle fat, beautify the hair with walnut oil, extract poison from an arrow wound with unripe cranberries, treat burns with birch bark, and substitute mother's milk with hickory nut paste. Some of these practices were so effective and quick that in later years certain devout Puritans suspected the work of Satan.

Despite the seeming simplicity of its technology, North American civilization was far larger and more organized than the Europeans ever knew. The explorers of the sixteenth century had brought European germs that wiped out a huge portion of the population, not only on the coast but along the rivers of the Mississippi watershed. Disease killed at least a third of the people in New England, maybe three-quarters. Many decades later, when the first settlers arrived, they found a thinly populated continent. They simply assumed that the population had never been any larger. They had no idea that the people around Cape Cod had jewelry made of copper mined in the Great Lakes region, that corn from Virginia made its way to Maine, that seashell beads beautified women in Wisconsin and the Dakotas.

The settlers at Plymouth never identified the Wampanoag by that name. Though an earlier explorer, Adrian Block, had called them "Wampanoo," the first settlers knew them as Pokanokets. They occupied the area that would later be known as eastern Rhode Island and southeastern Massachusetts. The Nauset on Cape Cod were allied with the Pokanoket and later became part of the Wampanoag group. The Wampanoag tribes also lived on the islands south of the cape that would come to be known as Martha's Vineyard and Nantucket. Pokanoket means "Place of Clear Land." Wampanoag means "People of the East" or "People of the Dawn." An estimated 21,000 to 24,000 People of the Dawn lived in the area when the strangers sailed in from the east.

The People of the Dawn lived modestly, little interested in the kind of technological and architectural achievements that Europeans would consider great. Jewelry of polished seeds, copper chips, feathers and mother-of-pearl satisfied their need for personal beautification, at least until the Europeans arrived with dazzling beads of glass. Extended families — parents, children, aunts an uncles, grandparents, as many as fifty in all — lived together in long, narrow houses with rounded roofs. A long house would have as many as four fireplaces in a line down the center. A house was a *weetoo*. A house of three fires was a *nisweetoo*. A house of five fires was an *abbonaweetoo*. The smoke of the fires rose through holes in the roof that could be closed with mats in times of heavy rain. The People slept on piles of furs on raised platforms of sticks along the walls. They could make a long house from a single piece of bark separated from a tree several paces in circumference. They cut the bark in the spring, when it was soft with sap. A simple frame of bent green sapling poles, lashed with sinews of bark and roots from cedar trees, supported the bark from the inside. They could also overlap smaller pieces of bark as shingles. Walnut bark was especially good for shingles. Evergreen roots were especially good for sewing them into place. They insulated the walls with mats of woven reeds sewn with roots and cedar bark pulled by a long sliver of the leg bone of a crane. The hollow reeds held the heat well. The houses stayed warm on the coldest nights.

People moved with the seasons. In the spring, some would go live near the sea, where they could gather lobster, crabs, shellfish, and the fish that came into streams to spawn. During this short period, they slept under the stars.

In the summer, families dispersed to live near their

fields. There they built smaller houses for the growing season. The summer houses were round and about fifteen feet in diameter. In the fall, men went to hunt. By winter, families came back together in their long houses.

The Wampanoag built canoes from the same trees that supplied the bark. When they built a house, they built a canoe, too. They cut the trees down by packing mud around the trunk, leaving the lower part exposed. Then they lit a fire around it. The trunk burned until the tree toppled over. An Indian woman, it was said, could fell several trees with fire in less time than a European man could fell one tree with an axe. She could even take a nap while she was felling trees. They used fire to dig out their dugouts, too, then finished the job with stone tools. The bigger canoes, forty or fifty feet long, could hold forty men.

The men dealt with death, it could be said, while the women dealt with life. The men went out and killed things, and the women turned the dead things into food, clothes, weapons, and tools. They used deer bones, clamshells, and stones to scrape the hair and flesh from hides. They used the brain of the animal to tan the hides, stretching and pulling the hide as they slathered it with gray matter. They sewed the clothes and moccasins using the tendons of the deer for thread, splinters of the foreleg for needles.

Europeans had an unfair perception of the Indian divisions of labor. By all appearances, the women were doing most of the work: tending the fires, cooking the food, grinding the corn, tending the fields, weaving mats, carving utensils, tanning pelts, and sewing clothes. Little girls served as scarecrows in the fields. Europeans saw the men having a good time hunting and fishing. Those were sports in Europe, of course, while in Indian country they were livelihoods. Hunting deer involved putting up a long fence of posts and felled trees that guided the prey into an ambush of men with spears. Fishing might involve a precarious hunt in a canoe in the dark, holding torches over the water and hurling harpoons at sturgeons and blackfish. A mistake in balance or the harpooning of an oversized fish might land everyone in the ocean. Arguably the women had the easy life, sitting around sewing, carving, cooking, and talking while the men were working up sweat and risking their lives.

A chief ruled the tribe. The Wampanoag tribes knew their chiefs as sachems. The Pokanoket sachem — Massasoit, when the Mayflower arrived, and later his son, Metacom, who called himself King Philip — inherited the throne (or, more precisely, a pile of animal pelts) from a parent, usually a son from a father. In the absence of a son, a daughter would do — same rule that determined royal succession in Europe. Entitlement, however, was not carried solely in the genes. The sachem had to prove himself worthy. A tribe could oust him for poor judgment, cowardice, ignorance, or other lack of leadership skill. To remain worthy of his title, he had to keep the tribe in harmony with the spirits of nature. If the relationship between the tribe and nature went sour, it was his fault. The consequences could be anything from hunger to invasion. But as long as things went well, he was king. He ruled with a council of advisors who accompanied him everywhere to advise him and protect him.

Every year, the tribe paid tribute to the sachem. They brought him gifts of pelts, weapons, tools, and great supplies of food, especially corn. He would use this wealth to ensure that everyone had enough to eat and to make deals with other tribes. Basically, the annual tribute was a voluntary tax, and the tribal budget consisted of the pile of goods that the sachem collected.

The European settlers did not teach the Pokanoket about thanks-giving. In fact, the giving of thanks among Indians was as constant and ongoing as the manipulation and harvesting of nature. The taking of life, be it that of a clam or a chestnut tree, was a moment for a prayer of thanks. To fail to use any part of that life was something like a sin. They used all, wasted little, lived well, and didn't need a holiday to give thanks.

Chapter Seventeen

Early American Politics

A round the end of July, John Billington, mid-teen son of the man who had made opprobrious speech against Captain Standish, brother of the boy who had set off a musket aboard the *Mayflower* and later discovered the lake that would be known as Billington's Sea, followed his family tradition of trouble-making and got himself lost in the woods. Not even Squanto could track him down. The boy had wandered hard and fast in the wrong direction, living off berries until he arrived at an Indian plantation some twenty miles to the south. The place was called Manomet. The Manomets took him even farther away to a Nauset village.

Squanto asked around, and eventually Massasoit sent word that the young fool was alive in the hands of the Nausets. Governor Bradford called for a mission to retrieve the boy. With Squanto to interpret and his friend Tokamaha-mon to help out, several men took to the shallop and set off to the south under sunny skies. True to their luck, as soon as they got out to sea, the weather turned bad. Pounded by wind, rain, thunder, lightning, and even a waterspout, they barely made it to a harbor in the land of the Cummaquid, where they thought they might find young Billington. They anchored in the middle of the harbor and slept in the boat. When they awoke, they found the tide had pulled all the water from under them. Stuck 'till the moon came around with the tide again, they sent Squanto and Tokamahamon to talk with two Indians who were looking for lobsters close to shore. The lobstermen knew of the boy and said he was in Nauset, farther out on the Cape. They invited the English in to shore for something to eat, then took them to their chief, Iyanough, who the journalist described as no older than twenty-six, personable, gentle, courteous, cheerful, "Indeed not like a savage, save for his attire."

"One thing was very grievous unto us at this place," the journalist wrote. "There was an old woman, whom we judged to be no less than a hundred years old, which came to see because she never saw English, yet could not behold us without breaking forth into great passion, weeping and crying excessively. We demanding the reason of it, they told us she had three sons who, when Master Hunt was in these parts, went abroad to his ship to trade with him, and he carried them captives unto Spain (for Squanto at that time was carried away also) by which means she was deprived of the comfort of her children in her old age. We told them we were sorry that any Englishman should give them that offense, that Hunt was a bad man, and that all the English that heard of it condemned him for the same; but for us, we would not offer them any such injury though it would gain us all the skins in the country. So we gave her some trifles, which somewhat appeased her."

Chief Iyanough and two others joined them for the sail to Nauset. There the Indians went ashore to tell Aspinet, the chief of the Nauset, of their arrival and ward off any defense. Many Indians came to the beach. Among them was the man whose corn the settlers had confiscated back in November. The English explained and promised to pay, either returning with corn or holding it in Patuxet for him. He promised to come get it.

After sunset, Aspinet showed up with an entourage of a hundred braves. With them was young Billington, draped with beads. Fifty armed Indians carried him across the water to the boat while the other fifty remained on shore, bows in hand. The English accepted the boy and rewarded his saviors with a nice knife.

It was during this interchange that the English learned that the Narragansett had gone on the warpath and captured a Nauset. Concerned for the safety of Plymouth, they headed for home. The winds were against them, however, and they were running short of drinking water. They spent the night close to shore, where Iyanough soon showed up with most of his village's men, women, and children. They took a contingent of English a long way through the dark to a place with water, but there was something wrong with it. They couldn't drink it. Back at the shallop, women put on a little show, dancing hand in hand. Iyanough gave the English a necklace from his own neck and what water he had, and the shallop set off again. But the water wasn't enough. The winds held them back. When they pulled up for the night again, Iyanough again showed up. He got in the shallop and led them back to Cummaquid for water and some entertainment. Then the English sailed for home as fast as the wind would carry them.

Back in Plymouth they learned of a serious Indian political situation which under the treaty with Massasoit would involve the people of Plymouth. The Narragansett had indeed routed some of Massasoit's people from their land. Worsening the situation, a "petty sachem" under Massasoit, Corbitant, was trying to disrupt an alliance among tribes that would eventually become the Wampanoag. Long suspected of being a sympathizer who was "too conversant" with the Narragansett, Corbitant was reported to be in Nemasket, trying to persuade Massasoit's people to come over to his leadership. Corbitant was also slandering the settlers in Plymouth, "storming at the peace" that had been established among the settlers, the Pokanoket, the Nauset, and the Cummaquid. He was also maligning Squanto, Squanto's friend Tokamahamon, and Hobomok, an advisor to Massasoit who was living just outside the Plymouth palisade with his family, keeping an eye on the settlers, helping them get along, and reporting to Massasoit.

The Corbitant situation was treacherous stuff. If the Wampanoag tribes went to war with each other, Plymouth's pathetic little militia had to back up the Massasoit's people. If Massasoit lost the support of a few villages, the Narragansett could easily take control of the whole area. They might even go after the Nauset out on Cape Cod. The fifty-two people of Plymouth would find themselves surrounded, their backs to the sea, no ship to take them away, and no friends to come to their rescue. Would the new Narragansett neighbors prove as friendly and helpful as the Pokanoket? Not if Corbitant had his way.

The complexity of the situation rivaled the political machinations of Europe. The settlers probably knew only a fraction of what was really going on. All they knew was that they were backing a weak but deserving ally, that they might have to go to war to prevent a war, and that if they went to war, they would lose.

Tokamahomon went to have a talk with Corbitant, but Squanto and Hobomok would not go with him. Later, smelling trouble, they thought they'd better go see Massasoit. They hurried to Nemasket, but there the treacherous Corbitant and his henchmen discovered them and trapped them in a house. Corbitant could not have made a more strategic capture. By eliminating Squanto, he deprived the settlers of their tongue. Unable to communicate with Massasoit, they would have no idea what was going on. As allies, they'd be useless. In fact, they probably wouldn't be allies for long. Misunderstandings would feed suspicion, and suspicion would contaminate the relationship. To end the English invasion and ensure a Narragansett victory, all Corbitant had to do was slit Squanto's throat.

But first he had to deal with Hobomock. Apparently Corbitant's men had already taken Squanto away, but when they tried to deal with Hobomock, he fought back. Corbitant had a knife to Hobomock's chest, but he broke away and fled for Plymouth. There he reported, in broken English and horrifically graphic sign language, that Squanto had been captured and was probably dead.

With little or no reflection on the love-thy-enemy/turn-thy-cheek teachings of their Savior (none documented, anyway), the Christians resolved to assemble an army and march for Nemasket at sunrise. Their mission: revenge, pure and simple. The journalist used that word twice. They couldn't bring their beloved Squanto back from the dead, but they could sure even things out. They knew just how to do it. They would simply cut Corbitant's head off. If possible, they would also capture Nepeof, an ally of Corbitant, to be held hostage pending news of Massasoit. They intended harm on no one else. It was Corbitant they wanted. It was personal.

It was also political. They had a promise to keep. "If any did unjustly war against him, we would aid him; if any did war against us, he should aid us." Bradford wrote that "[Squanto's murder] was not conceived fit to be borne; for if they [i.e. the settlers] should suffer their friends and messengers thus to be wronged, they should have none could cleave to them, or give them any intelligence, or do them service afterwards, but next they [the Indians] would fall upon themselves [the settlers]."

On August 14, 1621, under the command of Myles Standish, ten rag-tag commandos set off on a fourteen-mile hike through a rainy dawn. Three or four miles from Nemasket, they pulled off the path to figure out what to do next. They decided on a midnight raid. They planned their tactics and encouraged each other. Captain Standish, the professional soldier, must have been aware of his army's limited experience in killing other people. Quite likely they never had. Now they were most likely going to have to. They were going into this Indian town to do what they had to do. They'd have ten or twelve shots before they had to reload. They couldn't afford to miss a target. They couldn't hesitate to pull a trigger. They couldn't shoot the wrong person and have the whole village turn against them. And after that opening salvo, they'd might have to resort to hand-to-hand combat against a superior force.

They set off into the night, Hobomok leading them through the forest until he got them lost in the rainy dark. A forest in New England in the middle of the night in the rain in 1621 was pitch black. A man literally could not see a hand in front of his face. They had no way to produce light without a complicated effort to make a fire that would have revealed their presence. Maybe a psalm-prayer helped: *Surely thou wilt light my candle: the Lord my God will lighten my darkness.* Or maybe the sky was lightening with the first glow of dawn. One of the settlers who had been to Nemasket — probably Winslow or Hopkins — figured out the way.

They arrived wet, weary, and discouraged. They ate what food they had, ditched their knapsacks and whatever else they didn't need for battle. Hobomok pointed out the house where Corbitant would be sleeping. They devised their tactics, probably a plan like the one Corbitant had used to capture Squanto, based on surprise and overwhelming force. They sneaked into the village, surrounded the house, and some of the tougher men burst in through the door to catch everyone asleep.

But Corbitant wasn't home. The people in the house, ripped from sleep, were too terrified to speak. The strange men in their house, with their guns and threatening gestures, were all but unintelligible. The terror broke down to pandemonium. Some people cowered in fear while others broke through a back door, injuring themselves, aggravating the scene with blood and screams of pain. Other people tried to appease the raiders, holding out food in their trembling hands. It was probably Hobomock who got through their panic with the message that they had come only for Corbitant. Where was he?

Torn between fear and the promise that the invaders had not come to kill them, they imparted that Corbitant and his men had left — and that Squanto was alive. A hurley-burley of confusion spread through the town. The English let off two shots just for the sake of terror. It worked. Boys squealed in the darkness that they were women, and women clung to Hobomok, calling him friend. Hobomok climbed up on a house and called out to Squanto and Tokamaho-mon. They had heard the shots and now showed up with several men, some of them armed. The good guys regrouped in the house and released everyone, telling them again that they were there for Corbitant and no one else.

Things calmed down by morning. After a search of the village, it was confirmed that Corbitant and friends had indeed fled. The Plymouth raiders went to Squanto's house for breakfast. They made it clear to everyone that Corbitant would not be safe, not even in an Indian village, if he continued to threaten them or their friends. The settlers had always treated him kindly and, until now, had never intended him ill. Furthermore, if Massasoit did not return from Narragansett in good condition, or if anyone threatened Squanto, Hobomok, or any Massasoit subject, the settlers would seek revenge and oust whoever opposed Massasoit. As for anyone who had been wounded in the raid, they were welcome to come to Plymouth for treatment by their doctor, Mr. Fuller. One man and one woman took them up on that offer. They, Squanto and Squanto's friends accompanied them back to Plymouth, where by God's good providence they arrived the next night, safe and sound.

The military intrusion had the political effect they had hoped for. "After this they had many gratulation from divers sachems, and much firmer peace," Bradford wrote, "yea, those of the isles of Capawack sent to make friendship; and this Corbitant himself used the mediation of Massasoit to make his peace, but was shy to come near [Plymouth] a long while after."

Chapter Eighteen

Summer

Summer found the settlers at peace with the people around them and in the good graces of nature. Bradford wrote that they were "all well recovered in health and strength and had all things in good plenty." They caught all the fish they could eat, traded trifles for oysters, and filled a hogshead with eels in a matter of hours. In just one day four men shot enough fowl to feed everyone for a week. They ate lobsters that weighed several pounds. They found three varieties of wild plums. They planted twenty acres of Indian corn, six of barleycorn. The barley grew "indifferent good" in the rocky soil, which meant little if any malt, which meant little if any beer. The fish trick worked well with the corn. Only the peas failed to produce. Planted too late in the spring, they blossomed but soon wilted under summer's sun. But no one complained of the warmth, at least not in writing. Edward Winslow later wrote, in a letter glowing with the optimism of a real estate agent, that he could not remember a more seasonable year. He compared the climate to that of England, but less foggy, warmer in the summer, maybe just a little colder in the winter. Given some livestock of heavier duty than goats and pigs, he wrote, "I make no question but men might live as contented here as in any part of the world." The Bible described the situation well: *He watereth the hills from his chambers: the earth is satisfied with the fruit of thy works. He causeth the grass to grow for the cattle, and herb for the service of man: that he may bring forth food out of the earth...*

Over the next two years, they would develop a tradition for going to the meetinghouse at the fort each Sabbath. They took their muskets, just in case. Though they never had occasion to do so, a given Sabbath could have found them praying one moment, shooting cannons out the windows the next.

A description by a visitor six years later described the Sabbath call to meeting.

"They assemble by beat of drum, each with his musket or firelock, in front of the captain's door; they have their cloaks on, and place themselves in order, three abreast and are led by a sergeant without beat of drum. Behind comes the Governor, in a long robe; beside him on the right hand, comes the preacher with his cloak on, and on the left hand, the captain with his side-arms and cloak on, and with a small cane in his hand; so they march in good order, and each sets his arms down near him. Thus they are constantly on their guard day and night."

They dressed for the occasion, putting on their Sunday-go-to-meeting black-and-white best. They held meeting in two sessions each Sunday, one in the morning, one in the afternoon, each lasting a good three hours or so. Sometimes they met on a weekday to hear a sermon. They filed into the meetinghouse, men to one side, women and children to the other, a distribution they called "dignifying the meeting."

They had no ordained minister at Plymouth and thus no one with the title of Pastor or Teacher. They had to get by on an Elder, William Brewster. As a layman, he could not administer sacraments or define doctrine. As the highest-ranking church figure, however, he ruled over the congregation. He led the worship. He preached within his limited capacity. He taught the young and inquisitive a thing or two. He kept an eye on the moral situation, and he admonished those who strayed from the straight and true. The community had no room for error in the eyes of God.

The Plymouth church had had two deacons, at least for a while, but John Carver's death left Samuel Fuller alone in that capacity. As deacon, he collected offerings and saw that the poor and elderly were taken care of — easy responsibilities in that first year at Plymouth, when everyone was poor, no one had anything to offer, and William Brewster was the only person who could qualify as elderly. Still, Fuller tended the sick and no doubt did what he could to help everyone in that terribly difficult year.

The opinions of the Elder and the Deacons figured heavily in church decisions, but the Separatist church recognized the power of the congregation, or at least the men in the congregation, or at least those men who could claim to be head of a household. Wives, children and servants, in other words, would have to register their opinions at home and hope their head of household would represent them in town decisions.

During church service, men could express opinions, contribute to discussions of theology, and confess confusion. Sometimes Brewster would deliver "prophesies," reading a few lines of scripture, then explaining a bit about the passage, then opening the issue to discussion. With the pastor's permission, a man could stand up and express his thoughts on the issue for as long as he felt necessary. After each man had said his piece, Brewster would correct any errors, then accept questions from the men of his flock. Women, children and servants would keep respectful silence except to sing psalms and say "Amen." They sang psalms in melody only and without instrumentation. They had no foreordained posture for prayer. They might sit, stand, or kneel, depending how the spirit moved them.

Until the fort on the Mount was finished, church was held in the common house, or maybe even outdoors. "Church" was the phenomenon of the congregation, their beliefs and worship. The building where it happened was called the "meetinghouse." When church wasn't in session, it might well be used as a courthouse or a school or even a jail. In fact, church might have met in someone's residence. If it had pews, they were simple benches. Maybe people brought chairs. Maybe they stood. We don't know. It's possible the meeting house was configured like some New England churches in later years, with pews running the long way across the rectangular space, putting everyone nearer the pulpit. But we don't know if they actually had a pulpit. We do think they probably had a communion table. We're sure the space was free of such papal distractions as paintings, statues, crosses, crucifixes, icons, and stained glass.

They knew the Lord's Prayer but did not necessarily recite it verbatim or recognize it as either a prayer or as something dictated by the Lord. They just kept it in mind as a kind of model. According to Matthew 6:9-13 of the Geneva Bible, the Lord's Prayer went like this: "After this manner therefore pray ye: Our Father which art in heaven, Hallowed be thy name. Give us this day our daily bread. And lead us not into temptation, but deliver us from evil: For thine is the kingdom, and the power, and the glory, for ever. Amen." Margin notes defined "daily bread" as "That which is suitable for our nature for our daily food, or such as may suffice our nature and complexion." Notes defined "evil" as "the devil, or all adversity."

They prayed in faith but also with a certain foxhole desperation. It's hard to imagine a community with more to fear. Though they'd made peace with some of the local people, they knew the potential for conflict. Outnumbered by over a hundred to one, they never stopped strengthening their fort. They also feared attack by the Spanish, who still claimed the Americas and whose inquisition of infidels hadn't quite ended. They feared the Dutch, who had claimed land from Manhattan to Cape Cod. They feared the French, who had colonies from Nova Scotia to Rio de Janeiro. They feared pirates, who might be interested in anything from gunpowder to women. They feared their own King James, who at any time could send a force to arrest them for improper religious practices. They feared hunger. They feared the illnesses of the previous winter returning to kill more people, maybe even kill everybody. They feared diseases that they hadn't seen since they left Europe — smallpox, measles, tuberculosis, leptospirosis, bubonic plague. They feared whatever it was that had killed the former inhabitants of their land.

They feared retribution from God for sins they had committed, feared their own inevitable tendency to sin. They feared Hell and had no hope of a Purgatory for those of forgivable sin. They feared Satan, feared his appearance as a dark man or a black dog, feared the classic image of him with horns, hooves, and pointed tail. They feared wolves, bears, rattlesnakes, copperheads, water moccasins, and spiders. Though there were no hyenas or lions on that side of the ocean, they feared them. They feared the infections of simple injuries, the crippling of common accidents. They feared lightning. They feared roof fires any higher than a man could fling a bucket of water. They feared the disasters portended by the passage of a comet, like the one that passed in 1607, the disastrous first year of the Jamestown colony. They feared the magic of witches in cahoots with the devil, maybe even the curses brought down by the conjurations of heathens in some dismal swamp. They feared the wrath of God. They feared the dark.

They must have feared the ghosts of their own memories.

Everyone had seen several friends die that previous winter, and almost everyone had lost a family member. Some had lost all family members. Only the Hopkins, Brewster, and Billington families survived in their entirety. (Actually, it is not known when the youngest of the Hopkins family, Damaris and Oceanus, died. One or both died by 1623, so it's possible they did not survive that first year at Plymouth.) No other family had both mother and father living. Of the forty-one men who signed the Agreement & Association, only nineteen still lived. Eight children who had come with at least one parent now had none. Of eighteen adult women, only four had survived. Almost everyone had lain sick for days just a few feet from the frozen corpses of people who had died with similar symptoms. They'd seen these friends and family members taken from the *Mayflower* and lowered to the shallop. Now, in spring and summer, they dug into the earth to plant seeds within a few hundred yards of the unmarked graves where their friends and family lay.

No one wrote in much detail about how they felt after this onslaught of emotional traumas. We can only imagine how they felt, what they remembered, and what they imagined as their own future. They might have been fortified by the harsh reality of the times. Untimely death had not been uncommon back in Europe. Few people reached adulthood without seeing siblings or parents die. In fact, most of the settlers had lost close family members even before the *Mayflower* set sail. But even the worst of plagues had not taken half the souls of an entire population. The stress of such loss and the implications for the future would terrify anyone. No doubt the certainty of God's love alleviated some of the mental anguish. Not much else could have prevented the psychosis that would have afflicted people less accustomed to untimely death and less sure of an afterlife.

Hard work may have helped, too. They had but one summer — just four or five months — to prepare for winter. They had no ship in which to take refuge. They had no piles of seasoned firewood, no stores of food. They had no time to spare. Over the course of the summer they built seven dwellings for families and four buildings for common use. At some point that year, maybe as they planned the town, maybe after they'd built these seven houses, William Bradford drew a crude map showing seven plots, all on the south side of "the streete." The map showed garden plots for Peter Brown, John Goodman, and William Brewster on the east side of the "high way" that went from the street to the town brook. John Billington, Isaac Allerton, Francis Cooke, and Edward Winslow had plots on the west side. Most likely all these families had houses that first year. Brown and Goodman had plots, but, being single, would not have had their own houses. Sometime that year the Governor's house would be built on the north side of the town's only intersection. By March, the Hopkins family had built a house. Later that year, Edward Winslow would write that the town had seven dwellings. These buildings would have to shelter everyone through the upcoming winter.

They planted their kitchen gardens in raised beds narrow enough for the gardener to lean in to the middle from the side, and as long as their lots allowed. Here they grew their smaller foods: endive, radishes, thyme, parsley, mint, sage, savory, sorrel, spinach, lettuce, cabbage, garlic, basil, borage, red carrots, yellow carrots, cucumber, thyme, Alexander, angelica, asparagus, blessed thistle, burnet, chervil, clary, colewort, chicory, fennel, hyssop, leeks, mallow, marigold, marjoram, summer squash, purslane — whatever seeds they had brought from England, the kinds of things most likely to get tossed into pots of soup. The bigger foods, the ones of heavier sustenance — the onions, parsnips, turnips, and corn — grew in the fields outside the village. Depending on which seeds the Pokanoket shared with them that first year, the settlers may have planted the fields with squash, pumpkin, watermelon, beans, sunflowers, or tobacco. Whether they got all these things planted in 1621, we don't know, since they didn't meet the Pokanoket until spring.

They planted gardens and fields but harvested a lot of

their food from nature, especially that first year. Squanto had arrived just in time to introduce them to the delicacy of tender skunk cabbage shoots and the bitter, chewy fiddleheads of unfurling ferns. He pulled cattail roots from marshes. He showed them the tubers of a sunflower the settlers called Jerusalem artichokes. They already knew about the little tubers called ground-nuts, the slender shoots of wild chives, the fragrant leaves, seeds, and roots of wild garlic. They made a curative tea from sassafras roots and black birch twigs.

They spent that summer waiting for their ship to come in. How many times did they look up from their work to check the eastern horizon for sails? So much hope from a sea so unpredictable! They had no way to know whether the *Mayflower* had made it back to England. If she hadn't, no one would know where to find them. The supplies and new people they needed so desperately might never arrive. Even if a supply ship left port and made it across the ocean, it would search for the colony not at Cape Cod but where it was supposed to be — somewhere between Chesapeake Bay and the Hudson. And even if the *Mayflower* had indeed made it back to London, there was no guarantee that the group of investing Adventurers would send supplies. The *Mayflower's* arrival with a cargo of rocks and air certainly wouldn't encourage further investment. The settlement outside the Virginia Company patent made support even more questionable. For all anyone knew, the next day might bring a fleet of ships bearing hordes of eager settlers and tons of fresh supplies. But it was far more likely that the last months of the year would bring nothing at all. Just as surely as they kept checking the horizon, they kept turning back to the earth to coax up what they could before the first frost. They couldn't mope in the shade. They had to worry while they worked.

They had no school that first year and probably no one made a concerted effort to educate the children. In some cases, parents may have taken time to teach their children the alphabet or encourage them to read the Bible. William Brewster would eventually have a collection of four hundred books that included the works of Aristotle, Machiavelli, and Francis Bacon, and treatises on everything from medicine to silkworms. Some, but not all, probably came on the Mayflower. Maybe a teenager had the energy, initiative, and curiosity to try to read from whatever classics he had available. More likely, the children of that first summer did not have the luxury of learning anything beyond survival skills. They learned by doing something useful, something that would help the community survive the next winter. They learned weed from herb, mushroom from toadstool, cranberry from nightshade, wild food from toxic temptation.

Of the one hundred and two passengers who had sailed from England, these were the survivors who saw the summer of 1621: John Alden, William Bradford. Isaac Allerton and his children: Bartholomew, Remember and Mary. John and Eleanor Billington and their sons, John and Francis. William and Mary Brewster, their sons Love and Wrestling, and their adopted boy, the bastard Richard More. Mary Chilton, an orphan at fourteen. Francis Cooke and his son John. Elizabeth Tilly (an orphan at thirteen) and her infant cousin, Humility Cooper. John Crackstone. Francis Eaton and his infant son Samuel. Doctor Samuel Fuller and his nephew, of the same name. Richard Gardinar. John Goodman and his buddy Peter Browne. Stephen and Elizabeth Hopkins and all of their children: Constance, Giles, Damaris, and little Oceanus. Also, their two servants: Edward Doty and Edward Leister. Priscilla Mullins. Joseph Rogers. Henry Samson. George Soule. Myles Standish. William Trevor. Richard Warren. Susanna White, her five-year-old son, Resolved, and infant son, Peregrine. Edward Winslow and his brother, Gilbert. A fellow known today only as Mr. Ely. The Carvers' three servants, Desire Minter, a girl named Dorothy, and John Howland survived the winter but were unemployed in May, when the last of the Carver family died.

Chapter Nineteen

To the Land of the Massachusetts

On September 18, ten settlers, Squanto, and two of his friends set out to meet the Massachusetts. Though the tribe had threatened the Plymouth settlers — at least that's what the Pokanokets had said — the settlers wanted to meet them and make peace. One good way to befriend enemies would be to do business with them. The Massachusetts had pelts. The settlers had utensils of steel, fabric of thread, and trinkets of glass. Maybe they could make a deal that would ensure — and depend on — mutual survival.

To take advantage of the tide, they set out in the shallop at midnight. They expected a short sail up to Massachusetts Bay, hoping to arrive that morning. But the trip of twenty leagues — about sixty miles — proved too far to go in a day. After bobbing around the bay for almost twenty-four hours, they dropped anchor the next night. They slept in the boat until morning, then went ashore. There they found a pile of lobsters on the beach, the catch of some Massachusett lobstermen. But they were Pilgrim lobsters now. The explorers gathered them under a cliff and sent two men up top to watch for trouble. Myles Standish, an Indian guide, and four other men went to look for people. They met a woman coming for her lobsters. They gave her the good news that she had just sold those lobsters, and they paid her enough to content her.

The woman told them where they could find some Massachusetts. They sent Squanto ahead to introduce the approaching visitors. The rest went back to the shallop to bring it in closer to the tribe.

They found a sachem named Obbatinewat, an ally of Massasoit, a man with problems. He was scared and on the run. The Taratines — a tribe later identified as the Abnakis — were after him. They controlled all the lands from Casco Bay, Maine, up to New Brunswick. It was a hard place to grow crops, so in the fall they ventured south to steal corn. Obbatinewat was also afraid of the "squaw sachem" of the Massachusetts. She, too, was after him.

This was a perfect opportunity to make a pitch for the

power of King James. By submitting himself to the rule of the great English king, Obbatinewat would receive protection. Perhaps imagining that Standish and his company had a vast army behind them somewhere, the beleaguered chief agreed to accept their protection. With England on his side, he agreed to take the visitors to the squaw sachem. She and her people were on the other side of the bay.

It took the rest of the day to cross the bay, which the journalist noted was large and had at least fifty islands. Some islands had been cleared and recently inhabited, though the people had either died or moved away. Two rivers fed into the bay. As a harbor, it was even better than Plymouth. It had rocks at the entrance that suppressed waves and supported fish.

It was dark before they arrived at the turf of the squaw sachem. The Indians went ashore to see if anyone was about. They found no one, but that didn't mean no one was around. The group spent another night in the safety and discomfort of the shallop.

Come morning, all but two men went ashore. They walked three miles to a place where corn had recently been harvested. They saw a house that had been pulled down, but they saw no people. A mile farther on, atop a hill, they found an unusual house on stilts. Nanepashemet, deceased king of the Massachusett, had once lived there. In a valley nearby was his fort: a ring of poles thirty or forty feet long stuck in the ground. A chest-deep trench ran round the fifty-foot circumference. The only way in was over a bridge. In the center of the fort stood the frame of a house. There Nanepashemet lay buried.

A mile farther on, they found another fort, this one on a hill. Here, they learned, Nanepashemet had been killed. No one had lived there since his death. The English waited there while two Indian companions went ahead to advise people of their approach. A mile farther on, they found women and a heap of corn. Apparently the women had been fleeing the English, pulling down their houses, hiding corn as they went, and hauling what they could. When the party caught up with them, the women feared the strangers but soon softened to their gentle behavior. They then shifted from flight and fear to hospitality and entertainment. They boiled some cod and other food. The journalist leaves us wondering how, despite the haste of their flight, they had cod, kettle, water, and fire. After a while, one of their men showed up, trembling with fear. The English soothed him and turned the talk to business. They had lovely imported trinkets to trade if he had a few common pelts. He did, and the trade was made. As for the squaw sachem, she wasn't around.

Squanto didn't like these people. He said they were

bad people who had threatened the people of Plymouth. He wanted to "rifle the savage women" and take their pelts and anything else of value. Christian values and English business sense prevailed, however. They said that these particular savages had never wronged them, and they didn't want to give the savages reason to wrong them in the future. They would deal fairly for skins, but if the Massachusetts ever just once attempted anything against them, the people of Plymouth would deal with them far worse than they'd ever been dealt with before.

They struck a deal right there. The journalist does not tell us how the buyers paid, but it must have been a good deal. The women carried the goods back to the shallop, then "sold their coats from their backs, and tied boughs about them, but with great shamefacedness (for indeed they are more modest than some of our English women are)."

The English promised to return. With a fair wind and light moon, they set out at evening and by noon arrived at Plymouth. There was talk about how nice the land of the Massachusett was, how perfect the harbor, how maybe they should have settled there. But no: it said right there in Deuteronomy 32:8 that God set the bounds of all nations. The Massachusett got their land, the newcomers got theirs, and in Plymouth they would stay.

Chapter Twenty

Tabuttantam

The English came to Plymouth expecting to meet blood-thirsty savages, and the Wampanoag tribes had every reason to expect the same from English ships. Both peoples expected violence. Both could have justified preemptive strikes. Yet not one word of *Mourt's Relation* or Bradford's *Of Plymouth Plantation* expressed disrespect for the people whom the English met in America. Granted, their use of the word "savage" implied a certain unconscious assumption that these were a different *kind* of people, but all judgmental references in these documents are complimentary. They use the words *strong, honest, generous, cooperative, valiant, courteous, gentle, fair-conditioned,* and *personable.*

In a letter to friends in England, Edward Winslow called them "trusty, quick of apprehension, ripe-witted, just." Despite the skirmishes in the first few weeks, the two peoples had never really hurt each other. They had held their fears and suspicions in reserve, and accepted risk in the name of not just political exigency but, in short time, an extraordinary friendship.

Sometime in the first half of the autumn of 1621, the settlers and Pokanoket shared a feast. We know about this event from a few sentences in a letter Edward Winslow wrote to friends in England a month later:

> *Our harvest being gotten in, our Governor sent four men on fowling that so we might after a more special manner rejoice together, after we had gathered the fruit of our labours. They four in one day killed as much fowl as, with a little help beside, served the Company almost a week. At which time, amongst other recreations, we exercised our arms, many of the Indians coming amongst us, and amongst the rest their greatest king, Massasoit with some 90 men, whom for three days we entertained and feasted. And they went out and killed five deer which they brought to the plantation and bestowed on our Governor*

and upon the Captain and others. And although it be not always so plentiful, as it was at this time with us, yet by the goodness of God, we are so far from want, that we often wish you partakers of our plenty.

The letter did not mention the dates of the event. It did not use the word "thanksgiving," or even "thanks," but Winslow's message to the folks back home all but wallowed in the accomplishment of plentitude. After a winter under murderous conditions, they had food. They had seven houses — not much space for 52 people but certainly better than a damp, leaky, drafty, unheated ship anchored off the coast. They also had four buildings for common use. They had friends. They had their God, and they were at peace with the peoples around them.

It's doubtful that the settlers intended to establish an annual holiday. They may have conceived the event for a combination of three reasons. For one, they had been in Plymouth for almost a year. November 11 would have been the day, but in all likelihood the feast took place between September 21 (when the shallop returned from the land of the Massachusett) and November 9. Michaelmas, a traditional celebration held on September 29, might have inspired a festival. Or they may have thought of having a feast as part of an *ad hoc* holy Day of Thanksgiving and Praise, a Puritan and Separatist celebration that was declared whenever God seemed to be cooperating with human endeavors. Or they may have simply decided a good harvest warranted a good meal. The harvest feast was an old English tradition that had little to do with religion beyond standard thanks to God for the harvest and the blessings of each day and each morsel of food.

Most likely the event started as a Pilgrim celebration, and when Massasoit's people came along, they were invited to join in. The presence of almost a hundred non-Christians at the feast, and Winslow's reference to "entertainment," would imply that the event was not the strictly religious Day of Thanksgiving and Prayer. Such entertainment may have included games, dance, songs, speeches, and revelry. The absence of any reference to November 11 or the end of a successful twelve months in America would hint that the celebration was not oriented around that fact or held that late in the fall. The traditional harvest feast is the most likely reason the settlers decided to do some extra hunting, break out the stored food, and invite the neighbors to share the food.

Only by conjecture can we imagine that first feast of thanksgiving in Plymouth. Mrs. Hopkins, Mrs. Billington, Mrs. Brewster, and Mrs. Winslow — the only adult English women north of Jamestown —served up a three-day meal for a hundred and forty people, ninety of whom had table manners different from those of Europeans. But the bare chests, the cultural differences, and the language barrier most certainly did not disguise the obvious: that these "savages" were good people who knew, without being told, the do-unto-others love that Jesus had spoken of. Though the Pokanoket had no word for "please," they did have one for "thanks" — *tabuttantam*. *Tabuttantamauaa* meant "he gives thanks." *Taubotenananawayean* meant "I thank you." *Tabutantamoonk* would be the closest known word to thanksgiving. It derived from *tampu-* (sufficient) and *–antam* (the mental sensation of being satisfied). In the small-talk of a three-day feast, the native and new Americans may well have taught each other these words. Then they probably used them a lot.

The four women had help — seven teenage girls and four family servants who could be put to fetching wood, drawing water, dressing game, building and setting tables, and generally helping to pull together an impossible feast for an improbable gathering. They put out the fixin's in a help-yourself buffet, with meats on wooden platters and stews in clay pots. The five deer brought by the guests were probably butchered into manageable pieces and either boiled or barbecued. Duck, turkey, wild goose, swan, cod, and sea bass were boiled in pots or roasted on skewers. The English would have eaten from their trenchers. As they could not have had enough trenchers for ninety guests, Indians may have been trencher mates with the English. Or the guests may have brought their own carved bowls, or, like the English, they may have just reached and grabbed a hunk of food and delivered straight to the mouth. Eating utensils included personal knives and wooden spoons, but not forks, which had been invented but not yet adopted by commoners. The English used large linen napkins, as often over the shoulder as in the lap, not only to mop the face and wipe the hands but to pick up hot food or secure a turkey or large piece of venison while carving it.

If the tables included the meat of domesticated animals, they would have been the excess males not needed for reproduction and not worth feeding all winter. The females would have been too precious for the litters they would produce in the spring. Apparently the hunters killed enough wild fowl that they would have no reason to kill their own chickens. They had plenty of corn to feed the fowl, so they might have let the roosters live until they needed them. Or they might have tired of the crowing and boiled the worst offenders until they were tender enough to eat.

The Pokanoket may have brought baskets of mussels, lobsters, oysters and clams. They may have brought a cod or a sea bass, gutted it, stuffed it with wild onions and wild garlic, run a stick from mouth to tail and roasted it over coals of hickory or sassafras. The Pokanoket may not have had a word for *gourmand*, but they knew how to eat. They may have brought wild grapes, walnuts, chestnuts, hickory nuts, ground-nuts, watercress, wild onions, crab apples, corn meal, and succotash. It was not the season of fresh berries, but the guests may have brought dried strawberries, gooseberries, raspberries, blueberries, and currants. They may have dried grapes into raisins. Without sugar, cranberries would have been too bitter to eat, though maybe a few, finely chopped, found their way into stuffings and porridges. We can only wonder whether the Pokanoket and English women shared recipes in a language that could not involve words. Maybe spontaneous culinary combinations brought forth dishes never before tasted in either culture. Canada goose rubbed with wild garlic seed and stuffed with cranberry-onion corn meal, watercress and walnuts? Why not?

The English women may have been familiar with turkeys because earlier explorers had brought some back to England for breeding. The women may have known a version of a recipe that would be published in England in 1623:

Take faire water and set it over the fire,
then slice good store of Onions and put into it,
and also Pepper and Salt, and good store of
the gravy that comes from the Turkie, and boyle
them very well together; then put to it a few fine
crummes of grated bread to thicken it; a very
little Sugar and some Vinegar, and so serve it
up with the Turkey.

The Indians had eaten turkeys, of course, not to mention the eggs of turkeys, as well as the eggs of ducks, geese and swans — but never the egg of a chicken. They had never drunk the milk of a goat or any other animal. They did not know the tang of cheese or the sweet fat of butter. They had never tasted cinnamon, nutmeg, mace, ginger, cloves, or black pepper. They had probably never experienced the effects of a gravy enlightened with parsley, sage, marjoram or thyme, and thickened with bread crumbs or egg yolk.

The English women may have made breads from their corn meal and, if they had any, wheat or barley flour. They may have raised the dough with whatever natural yeasts floated along — sourdough, in other words — then baked loaves in small domed ovens of clay. Or they may have cooked unleavened breads in skillets right over the coals. They may have baked berries or grapes into tarts.

They did not use the word "vegetable." They referred to sallet herbs, potherbs, and roots. The herbs and roots brought from England may have included parsnip, carrot, turnip, onion, cabbage, melon, radish, beets, and lettuce. These English herbs may have found themselves in stew pots with such American potherbs as pumpkin, squash, beans, purslane leaves, and wild plums. They may have brought from England the spices of India —cinnamon, nutmeg, mace, ginger, cloves, and black pepper.

Indian corn was of the flint variety, not the sweet kind that tastes good on the cob. It was best pounded and ground into meal, though the kernels could also be roasted until it puffed into something chewable.

Some or all the tables had tablecloths. Some of the people sat on benches. The more important men probably had chairs. The majority sat or squatted on rocks, logs, stoops, the ground, wherever they found space. Children and servants fetched food from other tables or passed bowls around. Beverages — probably just water, maybe beer if they managed to make any from their harvest of barley — went from hand to hand, lips to lips, around the table in wooden bowls. They did not drink coffee or tea, neither of which had been introduced to England. If they drank milk, it was goat milk, and only the watery whey left from the making of cheese. Maybe they still had a little aquavitae left.

They most certainly said grace. We can only imagine what the Pokanokets thought as their absurdly over-
dressed hosts closed their eyes, tilted their heads over their
trenchers, perhaps held hands, as the old sachem named
Brewster uttered unintelligible grunts and sighs toward the
sky. Those pious syllables undoubtedly recognized God
as Lord and Heavenly Father. They thanked Him for his
mercies, for the meat on the tables, for the nourishment
of life. They thanked him for letting none among them die
since spring. The thanks may have extended to include
the peace among peoples, the warmth of the summer, the
beauty of the fall, the bounty of the harvest, the increase
in the general well-being, and the strength that had followed the winter of starvation and mortality. They may have
mentioned the people who had not lived to partake of this
hard-earned bounty. They probably pleaded the humility of
those still doing God's work on Earth. Certainly they mentioned Jesus Christ, their Savior, and surely they must have
mentioned the other saviors, the ones who had come out of
the woods to save them. Maybe Squanto translated. If they
said something along the lines of the Lord's Prayer, Squanto may have translated with something that sounded like
Nooshun kesukqut wunneetupantamuch koowesuounk.
Peyaumooutch kukkeitassootamoonk. Toh anantaman ne

n-naj okheit, neane kesukqut. Asekesukokish petukqun-
negash assaminnean yeu kesukok. Ahquontamaiinnean
nummatcheseongash, neane matchenehikqueagig nutah-
quontamanóunonog. Ahque sagkompaguninnean en qutch-
huaonganit, webe pohquohwussinnan wutch matchitut.
Newutche keitassootamoonk, kutahtauun, menuhkesuonk,
sohsumoonk micheme kah micheme. Amen." Maybe Planters and Pokanokets all said "Amen" together, as if agreeing
on something. And then, by God, most certainly, they ate.

Epilogue

O n November 10 or 11, 1621, just a few weeks after the harvest celebration, a ship staggered into the harbor after a grueling voyage of four months. For the past two days she'd been at the tip of Cape Cod while her passengers tried to figure out where they might find Plymouth. She was the fifty-five-ton *Fortune*, the supply ship the Planters had so long awaited. She'd set sail just a month after the *Mayflower* arrived back in England. She had thirty-five passengers, among them Robert Cushman, the same who had felt death closing in on him fifteen months earlier. Bradford described this new bunch as "lusty young men, and many of them wild enough." He also implied that they weren't too bright. They'd brought no food, no beer, no supplies, and only three females, two of whom were married (one of them nine months pregnant), one of whom was just a girl. When this ill-prepared group saw the "naked and barren place" of Cape Cod, they figured they had the wrong place or that the people of Plymouth had already died or vacated. They didn't even want to get off the ship to look around. They were afraid the crew might just sail away and leave them there to die. They even considered taking some of the sails in to shore to force the ship to wait. But the master promised that if they found no one in Plymouth, he would take them to Virginia.

Bradford described the colony's disappointment.

> *So they were all landed; but there was not*
> *so much as biscuitcake or any other victual for*
> *them, neither had they any bedding but some*
> *sorry things they had in their cabins; nor pot, or*
> *pan to dress any meat in; nor overmany clothes,*
> *for many of them had brushed away their coats*
> *and cloaks at Plymouth [England] as they*
> *came. But there was sent over some Birching*
> *Lane* [i.e. cheap, pre-made, off-the-rack] *suits*
> *in the ship, out of which they were supplied. The*
> *plantation was glad of this addition of strength,*
> *but could not have wished that many of them*

had been of better condition, and all of them
better furnished with provisions. But that could
not now be helped."

The new people raised the Plymouth population to
eighty-seven, much better than fifty-two for planting crops
and defending the village, but much worse when it came to
spending a winter in seven houses already overcrowded.
Rations for the winter would have to be cut in half.

But the ship carried one useful and comforting item, a
piece of paper — a patent from the newly created Council
for New England Council, giving the settlers the right to
settle where they had settled. The actual grantee was John
Peirce, so the patent became known as the Peirce Patent.

The *Fortune* also brought a letter from wheeler-dealer
Weston, who, rather predictably, was upset over the *Mayflower's* delivery of nothing more precious than New World
rocks or whatever they used for ballast. He did not want
to know of difficulties. He expressed no sympathy for the
excruciating winter, the scores of dead, no understanding of
how the lack of a fishing boat had resulted in a lack of fish,
no grasp of the link between scant provisions and scant
production, no appreciation of the effort needed to scratch
up sustenance from land and fashion houses from a forest.
He blamed the Planters for lack of effort and demanded

something to show for his investment.

"I know your weakness was the cause of [the lack of cargo]," he wrote, "and I believe more weakness of judgment than weakness of hands. A quarter of the time you have spent in discoursing, arguing and consulting, would have done much more."

Bradford hit him back:

"But they which told you spent so much time in discoursing and consulting, etc., their hearts can tell their tongues they lie. They cared not, so they might salve their own sores, how they wounded others. Indeed, it is our calamity that we are, beyond expectation, yoked with some ill-conditioned people who will never do good, but corrupt and abuse others, etc."

Despite the poor faith evidenced by a supply ship without supplies, the settlers loaded the *Fortune* with pelts and clapboard and sent it back to England. The ship left within two weeks of its arrival. Her cargo was palpable proof of the Planters' worth, their hard work and good intentions, not to mention their courage. But fortune did not bless the *Fortune*. French pirates seized her and took her to France. There they stripped not only the ship of its goods but her passengers of their clothes. One of few American products to make it back to London, the only product of lasting value and by far more valuable than all that had been lost, was a copy of *A Relation or Journal of the Beginnings and Proceedings of the English Plantation at Plymouth, England.* Published as the anonymous *Mourt's Relation,* it became a best-seller. Not a penny of the profits or royalties, however, went to its authors.

Two ships, the *Charity* and the *Swan,* arrived in June, 1622, adding sixty more men to the colony. The men stayed in Plymouth for two months, then started their own settlement some thirty miles away. After a winter of cold, hunger, and problems with native people, most of them gave up and went back to England. Two more ships, the *Anne* and the *Little James* arrived in 1623. William Bradford married one of the passengers. Myles Standish married another, named Barbara. Of the ninety new settlers, sixty of them were in on the deal with the London Adventurers. The thirty others arrived "on their own particular."

In 1624, Edward Winslow went to England and returned with three heifers, a bull, and more settlers. The cattle were a big help, but they contributed to an increasingly complex financial situation. Plymouth now had more Planters to share a portion of the debt, which was good, but they also shared some of the assets that had been built at Plymouth. Meanwhile there were now private persons settling private property yet using some of the common assets that the original Planters had built, such as the church and the fort. Many Planters felt that the Adventurers had not contributed enough to satisfy their side of the original contract. Exactly who owned what and who owed how much to whom became too complex to calculate.

Meanwhile, the Adventurers back in London weren't getting much return on their investment. After various mishaps, continued bad planning, poor production at Plymouth, and increased religious strife between Separatist and Puritan values, the venture started breaking apart. In November of 1626, the Adventurers decided to cut their losses by selling their shares to the Planters. Under the deal, each head of a household could buy a share for each member of his family. In 1627, each head of household received twenty acres of land. They couldn't slice up their cattle, goats and pigs, so they formed groups of twelve or thirteen people who would share allotments of animals.

The shared debt didn't work out very well, so in 1628, eight men — Bradford, Standish, Allerton, Winslow, Brewster, Howland, Alden, and a *Fortune* passenger, Thomas Prence, formed a partnership that agreed to pay for the shares over the course of several years. They called themselves the "Undertakers." In exchange for their promise to undertake the debt, they received exclusive right to the colony's fur trade for six years. They finally settled the debt in 1642.

Little Richard Moore, whose parents had abandoned him and whose two sisters and one brother had died in the first winter, went on to become a sea captain. He married twice, not including a possibly bigamous marriage to a woman in England. He was accused not only of bigamy but of lasciviousness and gross unchastity with another man's wife. He was over eighty when he died.

William Latham, a boy of just eleven when he boarded the *Mayflower*, would grow up to break the peace and commit public drunkenness.

John Howland married the orphaned Elizabeth Tilley. They had ten children. When he died, he left his house to his wife and his land to his sons. His daughters got twenty shillings each.

William Brewster lived until April of 1644. "His sickness was not long, " Bradford wrote, "and till the last day thereof he did not wholly keep his bed. His speech continued till somewhat more than half a day, and then failed him, and about nine or ten a clock that evening he died without any pangs at all. A few hours before, he drew his last breath short, and some few minutes before his last, he drew his breath long as a man fallen into a sound sleep without any pangs or gaspings, and so sweetly departed this life unto a better." He was seventy-nine.

The infant Humility Cooper, after losing two sets of

parents (one back in England, one in the winter of 1620-21) was sent back to England. We don't know whether she was reunited with her mother back in Leyden. She apparently remained childless and unmarried, and died before she turned thirty.

Little Oceanus Hopkins died before he turned three. His father, Stephen Hopkins, continued to serve as assistant to the governor until 1636. Around that time he opened some kind of tavern, possibly in his living room. In 1637 he was fined for "suffering servants and others to sitt drinkeing in his house…and to play at shovel board and such like misdemeamenors," on a Sunday, no less. In 1638 he was arrested for selling beer for twice the going price. In 1639, he was fined for selling a mirror at twice the going price. He died in 1644. He left his son Giles a bull, his daughter Constance a mare, his daughter Deborah a black cow, a calf, and half a cow named Motley. To his daughter Damaris he left a heifer named Damaris, a white-faced calf, and the other half of Motley. To his daughter Ruth, he left a cow and a half, a calf, and a bull. To his daughter Elizabeth he left a cow named Smykins, Smykins's calf, the other half of Ruth's half-cow, and a heifer with half a tail. Son Caleb got his house, and his daughters got every "mooveable" good they could carry out of it.

Degory Priest's widow, Sarah, who had remained in

Leyden, came over in 1623 with a new husband and three children.

John Carver's maidservant, Dorothy, apparently married the widower Francis Eaton in about 1623 and died within a year.

John Billington, father of Francis (who had shot off a fowling piece aboard the *Mayflower*) and young John (who had wandered off into the hands of the Nauset) was accused (and acquitted) of conspiracy in a scandal of a sort too sordid to put in writing. He was hanged in 1630 for murdering John Newcomen. In 1636 Billington's wife, Eleanor, was whipped and sentenced to time in the stocks for slander. Two years later, she married a newcomer, Gregory Armstrong.

In 1656, Myles Standish, having survived unknown battles in Europe, the crossing of the *Mayflower*, the winter of illness and death, and confrontations with Indians, died in agony, apparently done in by a kidney stone.

Edward Doty survived the wounds sustained in his sword and dagger fight with fellow Hopkins servant Edward Leister. Leister soon left for Virginia. Doty remained in Plymouth to make trouble for the next thirty years. In 1632, he was sued for failing to hand over six pigs to fulfill a contract, then sued again for a fraudulent deal involving an exchange of bacon for beaver skins. He was fined an additional 50 shillings for calling the plaintiff a "rogue." In 1633, he was sued for slander, for failing to teach his apprentice enough, for breaking the peace, and for unspecified matters "raw and imperfect." He himself sued someone over a debt and received six shillings, six pence, and a peck of malt. In 1637 he was fined for assault. In 1641, his two cows and a steer devastated someone else's field of corn. In 1643, for reasons today unknown — his cows are suspected accomplices — he had to pay someone five bushels of corn. In 1647, he was sued for stealing trees. In 1650, his cows struck again. Five years later, he died.

Edward Winslow wrote several books and treatises, was elected governor of Plymouth three times, returned to England at least four times, and chose to stay there shortly after the English revolution, which ended in 1649. He died in the Caribbean sea in 1655 while on a military mission to free the island of Hispañola.

John Alden, the young man hired as a cooper for the voyage of the *Mayflower*, the only crew member who elected to stay in Plymouth, married Priscilla Mullins, now twenty years old, whose parents had died during that first winter. They had ten children. He served in various elected positions. He and Myles and Barbara Standish founded the town of Duxbury, where his house still stands. He died in 1687 at the age of eighty-nine.

Epilogue

A Standish son, Alexander, married an Alden daughter, Sarah. Their genes combined and went on to become vice president Dan Quayle.

William Bradford was elected governor just about every year for the rest of his life. In 1623, he married a newcomer, a widow named Alice (Carpenter) Southworth. Their wedding feast was reminiscent of the fall feast of 1621, with Indian guests bearing turkey and deer. He and Alice had three children. At some point, his son John, whom he and Dorothy had left in Leyden at the age of three, came to join him. Bradford took sick in the winter of 1656-57 and died on May 9. Typical of him, he left a will that was vague and trusting in the goodwill of others to distribute his worldly baggage in a fair manner. Two sons had already received land, and Bradford's will simply requested that the third "bee made in some sort equall to his brethern." Stock in Bradford's trading company was to be reserved for Alice's "comfortable subsistence."

Despite lethal political pressures from his own and neighboring tribes, Massasoit remained a friend of the Pilgrims until the end. Likewise, the people of Plymouth remained loyal to him. Robert Cushman later wrote, "The Indians are said to be the most cruel and treacherous people in all these parts, even like lions, but to us they have been like lambs, so kind, so submissive and trusty, as a man may

truly say, many Christians are not so kind and sincere...
they never offered us the least injury in word or deed."

During Massasoit's lifetime, neither the Wampanoag
nor the group at Plymouth broke the treaty of mutual assistance they'd signed in the hungry, desperate spring of
1621. In 1623, when Massasoit took terribly sick, Edward
Winslow cured him with an English potion. When the Massachusetts threatened war against the English, Massasoit
remained faithful to his treaty. But by the 1650s, Plymouth
was expanding into Wampanoag territory. Conflicts over
land and straying cattle were resolved in English courts,
usually to English advantage. In 1661, Massasoit died. He
was eighty. A hundred years later, he would be recognized
as "the wise, the just, the peace-loving, the true, the trusty,
the generous, the faithful, the constant, the warmhearted
friend of the Pilgrims."

Massasoit's son, Metacom, would not show such loyalty,
and he had little reason to do so. The Puritans who moved
into the area in the 1630s were less tolerant of the people
they were displacing. After a series of deceptive land deals
and invasions of Indian fields, Metacom, who came to be
known as King Philip, organized a war against the invaders. It started in 1675. A year later, the settlers, many of
whom refused to fight against their Indian neighbors, had
lost six hundred people and twelve villages. The English

killed three thousand Indians, destroyed innumerable villages and fields, sold captives into slavery, killed Metacom, drew and quartered his body, and displayed his head in a public square in Plymouth for a year.

Squanto turned out to be quite the cad. In 1622, exploiting his friendship with the English and his almost exclusive bilingualism, he tried extorting some of the local tribes. He told the tribes that the English were preparing to attack. He told the English that the tribes were preparing to attack. It was a dangerous game, greatly dependent on the human tendency to suspect and to let suspicion preclude communication. Fortunately, people on both sides figured out Squanto's ploy before somebody got killed. Bradford wrote, "...[the settlers] began to see that Squanto sought his own ends and played his own game, by putting the Indians in fear and drawing gifts from them to enrich himself, making them believe he could stir up war against whom he would, and make peace for whom he would. Yea, he made them believe [the settlers] kept the plague buried in the ground, and could send it amongst whom they would, which did much terrify the Indians and made them depend more on him, and seek more to him, than to Massasoit." Massasoit found out and demanded that the English hand over Squanto for appropriate justice — quite likely something along the lines of decapitation. The English were reluctant to turn over the man who had helped them so much, but they could not afford to lose Massasoit's good will. In a moment of incredible drama so typical of Squanto's life, the Pokanoket-Pilgrim show-down broke up as a shallop sailed into the harbor. It bore a letter from Thomas Weston, who, despite the letter Bradford had sent on the *Fortune*, was still annoyed that his investments weren't paying off. The excitement of landing the shallop postponed a decision on Squanto until Massasoit's messengers lost their patience and departed. Squanto stuck close to Plymouth after that. If Massasoit intended any revenge, his intentions turned moot by the end of the year, by which time, in a final and unwitting favor to his English friends, Squanto developed a nosebleed and died.

Plymouth Rock has had a few adventures since the Pilgrims established their toehold on the American shore. In 1774, pre-revolutionary patriots recognized it as a precious historical symbol that deserved a special spot on the Plymouth town square. With the use of large jacks and thirty yoke of oxen, the rock was hauled from its beachside bed to be lifted onto a carriage. But as it rose from the ground, it split in half, an inexplicable schism that hinted of a political schism that would come along in just a couple of years. The lower half of the rock was returned to its wet bed at the edge of the water. Oxen hauled the upper half of the

rock up to the town square, where for a while it was vener-
ated beneath a flag that said "Liberty or Death." Liberty
won out for most people, of course, but the rock was soon
all but forgotten. It became part of a wall that held up an
embankment in front of Town Hall. But people still remembered what it was. Bit by bit, souvenir hunters chipped off
pieces. Before it disappeared into thousands of pockets, the
newly formed Pilgrim Society built an iron fence enclosure
outside its Pilgrim Hall. In the attempt to move the rock, it
fell in front of the Court House and cracked. Even after it
was tucked into its fenced enclosure, people still managed
to chip off pieces until the town government finally cracked
down on the practice. Meanwhile, down at the beach, from
1859 until 1867, a stone canopy was constructed over the
lower half of the rock, which was still pretty much in its
original location. In 1880, the upper half of the rock was
reunited with the lower half, and "1620" was carved into
it. The rock, now cemented together, still resides beneath
the canopy at the edge of the water. Visitors are asked not
to touch it.

The *Mayflower* never returned to America. After dropping off the passengers, Master Christopher Jones sailed
the his ship back to England in just thirty-one days. Later
that year, Jones sailed her to France and returned with a
load of salt. It may have been her last voyage. In March,

1623, Jones died. In 1624, the *Mayflower*, assessed as *in ruinis*, was sold for the pittance of 128 pounds, eight shillings and four pence. Someone in Buckinghamshire claims to have a barn made of timbers from the *Mayflower*. For many years, myth held it that the masts of the *Mayflower* had become pillars in a chapel in Abingdon. It's not impossible that some of her became part of another ship. But in all likelihood, given the scarcity of trees in England, the *Mayflower* was taken apart, sawed up, and sold off as firewood. Once she dried out, she probably burned very well. After all, she was oak.

Acknowledgements and Bibliography

Many people have contributed to the accuracy and ideas behind this book. Jim Baker, curator of the Alden House Museum, contributed many facts, identified many errors, and illuminated the author's understanding of the times. Interpreters at Plimoth Planation inspired some of the dramatic yet factual presentation of information, and experts at that museum pointed out problems and offered facts and academic opinions. Correspondence with Caleb Johnson brought erroneous details to light, and his deep and careful research provided a wealth of information. Theodore Albert Rees Cheney edited the text with thorough professionalism. Christine Jablonski proofread with the eye of a writer. Gary Greenberg provided good advice. Solange Aurora Cavalcante Cheney supported the project all the way.

These are some of the sources used to research this book.

Abrams, Ann Uhry. *The Pilgrims and Pocahontas: Rival American Myths of American Origins*. Boulder, Col.: Westview Press, 1999.

Alden House Museum website. www. alden.org

Arenstam, Peter, et al. *Mayflower 1620: A New Look at a Pilgrim Voyage.* Washington, D.C.: National Geographic Society, 2003.

Atwood, William Franklin. *The Pilgrim Story.* Plymouth, Mass.: The Memorial Press, 1940.

Beale, David. *The Mayflower Pilgrims: Roots of Puritan, Presbyterian, Congregationalist, and Baptist Heritage.* Greenville, SC: Ambassador-Emerald International, 2000.

Bendremer, Jeffrey, and Deward, Robert. "The Advent of Maize Horticulture in New England," from *Corn and Culture in the Prehistoric New World.* Boulder, Col.: Westview Press, 1993.

Briggs, Rose T. *Plymouth Rock: History and Significance.* Boston: Nimrod Press, 2000.

Bradford, William. *Of Plymouth Plantation 1620-1647*, edited by Samuel Eliot Morrison, New York: Alfred A. Knopf, 1998.

Cline, Duane A. *Navigation in the Age of Discovery — an Introduction.* Rogers, Ark.: Montfleury, 1990.

Davies, Horton. *Worship and Theology in England from Cramer to Hooker 1534-1603*, Princeton, N.J.: Princeton University Press, 1970.

Bibliography

Deetz, James, and Deetz, Patricia Scott. *The Times of Their Lives: Life, Love, and Death in Plymouth Plantation.* New York: Random House, 2001.

Gorges, Sir Ferdinando, *A Brief Relation of the Discovery and Plantation of New England* [London 1622], Massachusetts Historical Society Collections, 2nd series.

Heinsohn, Robert Jennings, "Transporting the Shallop on the *Mayflower.*" *The Mayflower Quarterly.* September 2008.

Howe, Henry F. *Early Explorers of Plymouth Harbor 1525-1619.* Plymouth, Mass.: Plimoth Plantation and the Pilgrim Society.

Johnson, Caleb H. *The Mayflower and Her Passengers.* Xlibris, 2006.

_____. Caleb Johnson's website, www. mayflowerhistory. com

Karr, Ronald Dale, ed. *Indian New England 1524-1674: A Compendium of Eyewitness Accounts of Native American Life.* Pepperell, Mass.: Branch Line Press, 1999.

Mayflower II Little Compton, R.I.: Fort Church Publishers, 1993.

McIntyre, Ruth A. *Debts Hopeful and Desperate: Financing*

the Plymouth Colony. Plymouth, Mass.: Plymouth Plantation, 1963.

McPhee, John. "Travels of the Rock." The New Yorker,
February 26, 1990.

Mourt, G. (William Bradford and Edward Winslow) edited by Heath, Dwight B. *Mourt's Relation: A Journal of the
Pilgrims at Plymouth.* Bedford, Mass.: Applewood Books,
1963.

Nickerson, W. Sears. *Land Ho! — 1620: A Seaman's Story
of the Mayflower, Her Construction, Her Navigation and Her
First Landfall.* East Lansing, Mich.: Michigan State University Press, 1997.

Peterson, Harold L. *Arms, Armor of the Pilgrims 1620-
1692.* Plymouth, Mass.: Plimoth Plantation and the Pilgrim
Society, 1957.

Philbrick, Nathaniel. *Mayflower: A Story of Courage, Community, and War.* New York: Viking Penguin, 2006.

Pilgrim Hall Museum website. http://www. pilgrimhall.org

Pilgrim Plantation website. http:// www. plimoth.org

Plimoth Life. Vol. 4, No. 1. Plymouth, Mass.: Plimoth Plantation, 2005.

Price, David A. *Love and Hate in Jamestown: John Smith, Pocahontas, and the Heart of a New Nation*. New York: Alfred A. Knopf, 2003.

Russell, Howard S. *Indian New England Before the Mayflower*. Lebanon, N.H.: University Press of New England, 1980.

Salwen, Bert. "Indians of Southern New England and Long Island: Early Period." *IN Handbook of North American Indians. Vol. 1*. Washington, D.C.: Smithsonian Institute, 1978

Seale, Doris, et al. *Thanksgiving: a Native Perspective*. Berkeley, Calif.: Oyate, 1995

Simmons, William S. *Spirit of the New England Tribes: Indian History and Folklore*. Lebanon, N.H.: University Press of New England, 1986

Smith, John, edited by Philip Barbour. *The Complete Work of Captain John Smith (1580-1631)*. Chapel Hill, N.C.: University of North Carolina, 1986

The Thanksgiving Primer, Plymouth, Mass.: Plimoth Plantation, 1991

Versluis, Arthur. *Sacred Earth: The Spiritual Landscape of America*. Rochester, Vt: Inner Traditions International,

1992.

Weinstein-Farson, Laurie. *The Wampanoag*. New York: Chelsea House Publishers, 1989

Willison, George F. *Saints and Strangers*. Orleans, Mass.: Parnassus Imprints, 1945

Winslow, Edward. *Good News from New England*. Bedford, Mass.: Applewood Books, 1996

Wood, William. *New England's Prospect*. Amherst, Mass. University of Massachusetts Press, 1977

About the Author

Glenn Alan Cheney is the author of over twenty books, including novels, nonfiction, collected short stories, and books on controversial issues for young adults. He has also written hundreds of articles, op-ed essays, and poems. His travels have taken him through Europe, Africa, India, and South America, with much time spent in Brazil. He lives in Connecticut with his wife, Solange.